the
MODERN
DATING
workbook

the MODERN
»» DATING →
workbook

An INTERACTIVE
APPROACH
to finding your
TRUE LOVE

CREATE A SELF-
WORTH PLAYLIST

(while staying
true to
YOURSELF)

BLOCK YOUR EX!

LIST YOUR RELATIONSHIP
NONNEGOTIABLES

MOLLY BURFORD

ADAMS MEDIA
New York London Toronto Sydney New Delhi

Adams Media
An Imprint of Simon & Schuster, Inc.
100 Technology Center Drive
Stoughton, Massachusetts 02072

First Adams Media trade paperback edition September 2021

ADAMS MEDIA and colophon are trademarks of Simon & Schuster.

For information about special discounts for bulk purchases, please contact Simon & Schuster Special Sales at 1-866-506-1949 or business@simonandschuster.com.

The Simon & Schuster Speakers Bureau can bring authors to your live event. For more information or to book an event contact the Simon & Schuster Speakers Bureau at 1-866-248-3049 or visit our website at www.simonspeakers.com.

Interior design by Priscilla Yuen
Interior illustrations by Alaya Howard and Priscilla Yuen

Manufactured in the United States of America

1 2021

ISBN 978-1-5072-1666-8

*To my grandparents, with infinite
affection and admiration.*

*Granny Mary Lou and Grandpa Gil,
you showed me that true love is worth
six decades. You are proof of the power
of commitment, gentleness, humor,
and staying true to yourselves.*

*Grandma Thelma, you taught me love is not
one thing, nor does it come from one place.
You are proof that sometimes the greatest
love story is the one you share with yourself.*

*I am so lucky I am your granddaughter.
Thank you for the lessons.
Thank you for the love.*

CONTENTS

Chapter 3
PUTTING YOURSELF OUT THERE • 65

Chapter 4
"SO WHAT ARE WE?" · 111

Chapter 5
BREAKING UP F'ING SUCKS · 139

INTRODUCTION

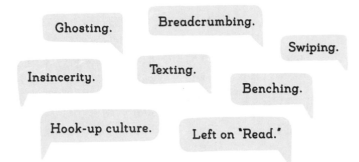

Ghosting. Breadcrumbing. Swiping. Insincerity. Texting. Benching. Hook-up culture. Left on 'Read.'

All together, these things make up modern dating. It's exhausting for pretty much anyone who has taken part. But when you are an overthinker or a deep feeler, it's even *more* difficult. If you've ever panicked after sending a text, if you've ever had your heart shattered by your own expectations, if you've ever felt as if you had to hide everything about yourself in order to be liked and approved of: Well, then *The Modern Dating Workbook* is for you.

This is a guide for dating in a modern world for the deep-feeling overthinker. With advice and ninety actionable lessons, this book will help you keep your head on your shoulders as you look for love. This book will serve as your reminder that it's totally okay to be authentically you. It's okay to tell some bad jokes because the right person will laugh along with you. It's okay to double text because the right person will triple text in response. It's okay to be messy and imperfect and to try a little too hard. It's okay to be too much, too there. Own it. Be *it*, whatever your *it* may be. The right person won't mind.

Dating is hard and probably always will be. There is always a chance of heartbreak, a little embarrassment, maybe disappointment. But, in the end, if partnership is what you truly want, then the stops along the way will be worth it. This book will be a resource for helping you on this journey. In the pages that follow, you will learn:

- ✔ *How to deal with situationships and almost relationships*
- ✔ *How to take it all a little less personally*
- ✔ *How to remember what you bring to the table*
- ✔ *How to fall out of love with an idea*
- ✔ *How to heal from breakups*
- ✔ *And more...*

Most importantly, though, this book will help you realize that you don't have to go against who you are in order to find and be worthy of love. In the end, you don't want anyone who doesn't want you. Real love, true partnership, doesn't need coaxing. It just needs you, the other person, and both of you showing up to do some loving, tender work. Pretending to be someone you aren't won't give you something real. But being who you are absolutely will.

So, take your time and trust yourself. Wait and see.

Love *is* out there. Go get it.

HOW TO USE THIS BOOK

Finding your person usually isn't a linear journey, especially during the Current Times. As such, you most likely won't be using this workbook in order. However, I recommend starting with Chapters 1 and 2. Chapter 1 covers preliminary dating stuff, like understanding what you actually want in another person, getting your head on right with empowered mindset shifts, and learning terms like *breadcrumbing* and *benching* and *ghosting*. Chapter 2 covers being single, which is technically where we all start. But after that? Simply skip around based on where you currently are. No one story is ever the same, so everyone will work through this guide a little differently.

Of course, it's always possible you *could* meet the love of your life right out of the gate and therefore *would* use this book in order. If so, I cannot relate, but honestly—good for you!—you can skip the breakup and almost relationship chapters. Also, you're welcome, because I'm sure this guide helped. I'd like an invite to the wedding. Please make it an open bar.

I'm kidding. Sort of.

Anyway.

You'll also notice the format is different from other workbooks. Each entry begins with an essay explaining a modern dating concept. After you read that, you'll be instructed to apply the lesson in an exercise. The point of each exercise is to help you in your journey to find love, gain confidence in yourself—no matter what—and own it.

Chapter 1

MODERN DATING BASICS

Understanding the Basics and Cultivating the Right Mindset

So, dating is on your mind, but you're not ready to get out there *just* yet. Maybe the idea of rejection makes you nervous, or apps sort of creep you out. Or perhaps it's because you're still overthinking a flirty text you sent that got left on "Read" at 8:42 p.m. in October 2018.

Whatever the case, you want a little time to prepare. This chapter will do just that and get you up to date (pun intended). From teaching you the latest vocabulary to showing you the ropes in cultivating the right mindset, this part is the prerequisite crash course before putting yourself out there. Sound good?

Let's get started.

OKAY, SO WHAT *IS* MODERN DATING ANYWAY?

Ah, love, a phenomenon that has both perplexed and enchanted humankind since the dawn of time. Okay...so maybe not the *dawn* of time, but close!

Love has been the subject of psychological research, the inspiration behind the majority of Taylor Swift's discography, and the feeling that poets have sought to put into words.

While the human need and desire for companionship hasn't changed, what *is* different is how we go about finding it. To sum up why dating has evolved would be impossible to do in one essay (or one book). One of the biggest reasons for the change is technology and its impact on communication.

We have so many avenues for staying in touch, with more created almost every day. This explosion of connectivity is both a blessing and a curse, especially when it comes to dating. After all, while there are ample ways to meet people to fall in love with, there are even more opportunities for love's exit. Dating has always been hard; technology absolutely makes it more confusing.

This is all to say that if you're feeling frustrated by modern dating and its intricacies, you're *so* not alone. You're not crazy for feeling over-whelmed; most of us are. Just remember, that's normal. It's not a sign you're doing something wrong; it's a sign you're doing something right, and that's putting yourself out there.

With the right mindset, patience, and ability to show ourselves as we authentically are, we can enjoy the ride, despite all the bumps along the way.

Do a Ten-Minute Freewrite about Your Experiences with Modern Love

In this activity, you're going to do a ten-minute freewrite about your experiences with modern love thus far. This will help uncover biases you may have to unlearn before putting yourself out there.

_____

_____

_____

_____

_____

_____

_____

_____

_____

_____

_____

_____

_____

_____

_____

_____

_____

_____

MODERN DATING TERMS YOU NEED TO KNOW

Technology has changed every aspect of life, including dating. The way we meet people and how we break up now is soooo different from when our parents met. My mom and dad were introduced through mutual friends. My friends and I use Hinge.

Because dating has evolved so much, a slew of new vocabulary now describes the trends the world has seen emerge:

GHOSTING *The brisk, sudden halt of communication with someone you had a thing with. No explanation given.*

BREADCRUMBING *When someone shows sporadic signs of interest via texts, likes on Insta, or random "We need to hang sometime!!" messages. However, "sometime" is actually code for "never." It's a way to keep you on the hook just in case. It makes you feel like shit.*

BENCHING *When someone likes you enough to keep you around but won't commit to you. You're an option, not the choice; aka benched, not unlike a third-string football player. (I don't know sports.)*

TALKING STAGE *(AKA MY PERSONAL HELL) A budding relationship in which you're in consistent contact, flirting, mutual interest, but that's about it. It's definitely deeper than friendship, but no one has made a move, at least not yet. The ultimate gray area, and not the fifty shades kind. Overthinking guaranteed.*

SITUATIONSHIP *A status more serious than casual but still less committed than a full-fledged relationship. You have the romance with a side of ambiguity. Research shows this is okay, as long as both parties are on board with it being fleeting, romantic but ultimately unattached.*

DTR *Defining-the-Relationship; aka time to commit (or walk away).*

Make Your Own Modern Dating Glossary

Those are the major terms, but what are some phenomena you've noticed? List and define 'em in the space provided. This exercise is helpful because putting names to things makes them less intimidating and easier to navigate.

TERM

DEFINITION _____

_____

TERM

DEFINITION _____

_____

TERM

DEFINITION _____

_____

TERM

DEFINITION _____

_____

TERM

DEFINITION _____

_____

TERM

DEFINITION _____

_____

♥ DATING APP 101

In October 2019, the Pew Research Center asked 4,860 adults in the United States about online dating. According to this study, 48 percent of the eighteen- to twenty-nine-year-olds surveyed reported using dating apps at some point. This statistic shows dating apps and websites, particularly among younger generations, are a well-known (and well-used) avenue for finding companionship. While this route definitely isn't for everyone, it is an option worth considering on your journey to find love.

To start, you need to know your first impression on the app is your profile. While what's included on your profile varies from platform to platform, there are some general key components:

★ Photos of you
★ What you're looking for
   (serious, casual, the will to live)
★ Interests and hobbies
★ Fun facts about you

Some apps, like Hinge, provide prompts for you to answer to show off humor, interests, and values. Sites like Match.com get into nitty-gritty details, like exactly what you're looking for, if you want kids, your childhood traumas, etc.

Online dating requires some trial and error to find the right platform for you. It helps to do your research. Talk to friends for their recommendations. And always practice online safety when dating. Meet in public places first, tell your friends where you'll be, and trust your instincts.

Plan Your Dating App Profile

In this exercise, you're going to plan out your dating app profile (or pro-files, as it doesn't hurt to have several accounts). On this page, answer these questions and plot out what you might want to share about your-self to potential dates.

What apps are you going to use? Why?

_____

_____

What photos would you use? Why?

_____

_____

What are your hobbies?

_____

_____

What kind of lifestyle do you lead?

_____

_____

What are your values?

_____

_____

What do you want potential dates to know about you up front?

_____

_____

IF DATING APPS AREN'T YOUR THING...

While dating apps are a popular avenue for finding modern love, they're definitely not the only route or right for everyone. There are a few reasons for this:

To some, online dating can feel completely superficial. After all, you're saying Y or N to someone based on pixelated photos and a few confessions.

To others, the number of options feels overwhelming. While there are plenty of fish in the sea, it can lead to decision fatigue and giving up on apps altogether. Just think about the Stanford Jam Experiment. It's like that but for choosing a life partner.

Whatever your own reason is for not really vibing with apps, it's possible to still meet someone in the outside world, aka Real Life.

There's the bar, cooking classes, and sporting leagues. How about an open mic night? A coffee shop? A concert even. There's also tapping into your friends' networks. After all, who knows you better than your pals?

Love is out there, both online and off. It all depends on your comfort level and preferences. Whatever route you choose is just fine. But, whatever journey you choose will require effort.

Love sometimes shows up when you're not looking. But sometimes, you have to do a little digging. Be brave. Put yourself out there. Talk to the cute person ordering a whiskey ginger. Strike up a convo at the bowling league (get it?). You're a catch. It's time for someone to reel ya in!

Brainstorm Ways to Meet People IRL

Alright, so if you're gonna try playing the IRL field, you need to think of some spaces you might meet like-minded individuals. Hobbies connect, after all. In the following bullets, list some potential spots you might find your S.O. Think about what your lifestyle is, who you'd like to meet, and so on.

★ _____
★ _____
★ _____
★ _____
★ _____
★ _____
★ _____
★ _____
★ _____
★ _____
★ _____
★ _____
★ _____
★ _____
★ _____
★ _____
★ _____
★ _____

WHAT LANGUAGE DOES YOUR HEART SPEAK?

If you've been on the Internet in the last decade, you've surely stumbled across the concept of a love language at one point or another. According to Dr. Gary Chapman, there are five love languages. They are the ways someone expresses and receives love. Dr. Chapman's five love languages are:

- ♥ Words of Affirmation
- ♥ Acts of Service
- ♥ Gifts
- ♥ Quality Time
- ♥ Physical Touch

You may not have just one. More often than not, there is a primary and secondary love language. So, for example, your primary could be Words of Affirmation, but you also value Quality Time.

Understanding our own love language is important before dating because you know what you need from a partner. Your future partner's love language may differ from your own, but that's okay. Because you can love them in theirs, and them in yours. It's all about awareness and communicating what you need.

Find Out Your Love Language

A number of quizzes online can help you determine your love language. In this space, theorize what your own love language might be, and why. Then, write out some ways you'd like your future S.O. to show that love language to you.

♥ ATTACHMENT STYLE 101

Attachment was first studied in the 1960s. Today, it continues to be all the rage online, with countless articles, quizzes, and videos about attachment theory and how it pertains to modern life and love.

Attachment theory defines four styles of attachment that are formed in childhood and follow us into adult life. They are:

- ♥ Secure
- ♥ Dismissive-avoidant
- ♥ Anxious-preoccupied
- ♥ Fearful-avoidant

Ideally, one is securely attached in their relationships. If you realize you maybe have a dismissive-avoidant attachment style or an anxious-preoccupied attachment style, that's okay. The good news is you can work to shift your thought patterns and behavior in a way that's healthier for both you and those around you. This includes your future S.O.

Tons of resources are available online and elsewhere to help you figure out your attachment style and work on it in a way that will eventually lead you to secure attachment. Try reading *Attached* by Amir Levine and Rachel S.F. Heller. It's a bestselling book on attachment as it relates to finding love. Check it out if you think you're having issues with attachment.

If necessary, it's totally cool to go to therapy to work out relational issues. Everyone struggles, and seeking professional help is nothing to be ashamed of.

Go forth and get securely attached.

Determine Your Attachment Style

There are endless quizzes online to help you determine your attachment style. Take one and write your results here. Then, think about how your particular attachment style affects your dating life.

TO THE OVERTHINKER WHO FEARS REJECTION

Here is a tough but liberating pill to swallow: You are not for everyone.

You're going to meet people who aren't interested in you in the same way you are interested in them. When it comes to romantic endeavors, it hurts.

Psychology has shown humans have a physiological response when perceiving a potential threat, such as social rejection. When this happens, the amygdala is activated; the primitive brain prompts either freezing, flying, or fighting in order to stay safe.

Let's apply this research to overthinking tendencies. When you over-think, you're trying to come up with every possible outcome or expla-nation to be prepared for "danger," such as romantic rejection. You do this by overanalyzing text punctuation, worrying if the last hug goodbye seemed forced, wondering why they called later than they promised. If you can see it coming, you can either cut ties first (flight), keep things as they are (freeze), or demand answers (fight).

Researchers recommend this approach: Acknowledge and then out-smart it. This helps calm the amygdala. Let yourself be afraid, and then go on your date anyway.

Dating will always have the risk of heartbreak. You can't control this, no matter how many scenarios you think up. View rejection as part of the process, not as an indictment of your character. It's okay to be fear-ful of rejection and hurt by it. What's not okay is letting that fear dictate your love life. In the end, this doesn't keep you safe. It keeps you lonely.

Redirect the Rejection

Some energies just don't mesh. Personalities clash. Values differ. Chemistry is absent. They might be a Sagittarius. Whatever the case, they're not the right fit. But you know what? Rejection can sometimes be a blessing in disguise. After all, when they let you go, you are free to find something else. Something real. Someone right for you, and for the person you find.

So, in this space, write about how this could be an opportunity, because it truly is one. What can you get out of the reroute? Where else can you go? Who else can you meet? (Hint: It's the person actually meant for you.)

_____

_____

_____

_____

_____

_____

_____

_____

_____

_____

_____

_____

_____

_____

ELEMENTS OF A HEALTHY DATING LIFE

Health is more than running on a treadmill and eating a salad. It also relates to the relationships we have with others, including romantic ones. In fact, it's been shown that our relationships directly relate to the quality of our lives. The quality of our relationships impacts our health, including our life span.

According to Healthline.com, a number of components signify a healthy romantic relationship. They include:

★ Shared values
★ Boundaries
★ Open communication (*both* ways)
★ Time apart
★ Flexibility
★ Compassion
★ Trust
★ Commitment
★ Physical intimacy

These elements will look different in every relationship, but ultimately are important to have. Before you start dating, think about how you'll gauge whether someone you're interested in dating seriously could make these elements exist within your specific dynamic. Communicate openly ahead of time about what you're looking for, what you need, and what their thoughts about these necessities are.

Write Your Own Building Blocks for a Healthy Relationship

The experts know a thing or two about relationship health, but you do too. On this page, write out some things you think contribute to a healthier relationship overall. Think about individual efforts, as well as the work you'll do with your partner as a team.

★ _____
★ _____
★ _____
★ _____
★ _____
★ _____
★ _____
★ _____
★ _____
★ _____
★ _____
★ _____
★ _____
★ _____
★ _____
★ _____
★ _____
★ _____

❤ WHAT'S YOUR CURRENT LOVE STORY?

I used to think love was something that wasn't going to happen for me. Ever since I was little, I had this sneaking suspicion I'd never find it. At one point, I even started convincing myself love wasn't something I even *wanted*. You can't feel rejection if it wasn't something you cared about in the first place, right?

I don't know where I learned this. (Maybe listening to far too much Taking Back Sunday at a young age? *JK, no such thing!*) But then I started being honest with myself, and in the past few years, I've had a change of heart (pun intended). I started being real with myself. I began to understand that wanting companionship doesn't make me weak. It simply makes me human. It's okay that I want love.

So, I literally had to start rewriting my narrative about love and unlearn unhelpful thought patterns related to dating. I had to tell myself a new story if I wanted a love story. My former belief system wasn't working.

What's the current story that you're telling yourself about love? What is your reasoning for why it hasn't happened for you yet? What has your experience with dating been thus far? What is the narrative you've applied to your love life? Is it healthy? If yes, then you can probably skip this section. But if you're like me, there's probably a chance you need to do a little reworking. And that's okay. Personal growth—we love to see it, don't we?

Rewrite the Narrative

On this page, write your current thoughts on love and what you feel about it. Then, rewrite it. Think of new ways to look at old feelings. Think about different narratives you can apply to the same experience. Be compassionate; be kind; be real.

GO FROM INSECURE AF TO EMPOWERED AS HELL

Infomercial announcer voice

Has this ever happened to you?

You're on a date with someone you're totally clicking with. You're attracted to them, but then the fear sets in. You don't know how they feel *for sure*. You could explore it. But you feel tempted to run out of the bar instead, never looking back to find out.

If this sounds familiar, then you might be dating from a place of insecurity. Instead of going with the flow, you mine for red flags, for reasons it'll never work, before it even gets a chance to begin. You time your replies to not seem desperate, even though you saw the text in 2012. (The "I was showering" excuse is not going to work now.) You squash any possibility of the Something becoming Something More.

Luckily, you can shift your dating mindset and become empowered AF. Here's how:

Hype up your nerves before a date with curiosity. Invite yourself to understand that not every outing will end in romance; you can still take something away from it, such as a lesson learned. A book recommendation that becomes a new favorite read. A fresh outlook on the world.

Most importantly, stop putting so much pressure on the outing. Do your best to not overthink what it could become. For now, it's just a date. Yes, it might evolve into a relationship. But at this moment, appreciate it for what it is. Take a deep breath, and see what happens.

Swap Insecure Energy for Badass Energy

Here are common disempowered mindsets. You're the editor. Cross out words, replace verbiage, and change sentence structures so they come from a place of power.

I am lucky they are even giving me a chance.

_____

_____

What are we going to talk about?

_____

_____

What if they hate me? What if I hate them?

_____

_____

Why aren't I enough?

_____

_____

I'm never going to find someone I click with.

_____

_____

DEAL BREAKERS AND YOU

What do you want in a partner? What would make you fall for someone else? Who's your dream person?

This isn't your *type*, per se, because our types often let us down and keep us trapped in a box, reliving the same dating experience over and over again. For example, mine happens to be tall men who need therapy. And that hasn't really worked so far, has it? No. No, it hasn't.

That's okay, because I'm trying a new approach and it's this: I will be focusing on tangible, *positive* traits that relate to how this potential person relates to *me*. For example, this person will:

★ Be considerate of my time
★ Understand my need for space
★ Have their own interests and hobbies
★ Be looking for something serious

It's important to have a general idea of your nonnegotiables ahead of time so you can identify potential deal breakers early on and not waste your time. You can catch yourself projecting. You can be mindful when looking at someone as they actually are, not who you want them to be.

Many people aren't going to check all of our boxes; in fact, most people probably won't. It would be unrealistic to expect someone to be perfect. (BTW, imperfections are the fun part!) However, there are qualities that you should stick to when looking for a partner. The first one? Kindness. Your partner should always be kind to you, no matter what. This is a baseline. If not, what the hell are you dating them for?

List Your Relationship Nonnegotiables

On the blank lines provided, list your relationship nonnegotiables—the essential pieces you won't feel complete without. Again, these won't be deal breakers but specific traits that draw you to someone romantically. Some examples include that this person:

★ Is kind above all else

★ Holds space for me

★ Listens well

★ Shares similar values

★ _____

★ _____

★ _____

★ _____

★ _____

★ _____

★ _____

★ _____

★ _____

★ _____

★ _____

★ _____

★ _____

★ _____

★ _____

YOU'RE NEVER GOING TO BE FULLY READY

Yes, this whole chapter was about prepping to put yourself out there. And, to a degree, it's okay to not be ready and ease your way into dating, especially if you just had a brutal breakup or honestly aren't emotionally ready. But the truth is this: You're never going to feel 100 percent prepared. It's about knowing when fear is just holding you back and not a valid concern.

So this begs the question: How do you know when your nerves are unfounded? Everyone's situation is different, but usually it's when your actions don't align with what you want. If you sincerely want to be solo, do yo thang! But if you want partnership but refuse to try dating apps because you're convinced no one will like you? Well, it's probably time to re-evaluate your behavior.

Eventually, you need to put the anxiety aside and meet someone for drinks anyway. You need to stop hiding your heart away because it's going to backfire and internalize those fears more.

You're never done growing. The trick is finding someone to evolve alongside. Trust the process, and learn to stop being afraid of the heat.

Rejection sucks. First dates bring butterflies. You have a tendency to overthink, but you can work at it *while* dating. You don't need to conquer all your quirks before someone else will love you. You don't need to be a specific size, have a perfect job, or be completely self-actualized.

Come as you are. The right person will always show up too.

Write about What You're Afraid Of

In this space, write about something you are afraid of, and then write out why it's okay. For example:

> I am afraid I will be rejected.
>
> Even if I am, one day, I'll be loved by someone who loves me back.

Now you try.

Chapter 2

EMBRACING SINGLENESS AND PRACTICING SELF-LOVE

Learn to Appreciate Where You Are and Understand That Self-Love Isn't a Destination

We all start out single in our journeys for love. And it's a status we may find ourselves back in from time to time. Modern dating isn't always a linear journey. It's not as straightforward as it used to be. There's no beginning, middle, and end; there are multiple versions of each.

Return to this chapter when you're single and when you're not. There is tons of advice on self-love here that's important whether you're solo or not.

HOW TO ANSWER THE DREADED QUESTION: "WHY ARE YOU STILL SINGLE?"

When a friend of mine used to go home for the holidays in college, her parents would ask, every damn time, "So, where's the boyfriend?" This irritated the hell out of her, but mostly it just made her feel sad and pressured, as it would anyone. It put a relationship as a signifier of validation, rather than her kicking ass in school and, frankly, life.

I'd argue the majority of the population has been asked *why* they are single at some point. It's so frustrating because it implies it's something to be ashamed of. Because the hidden word in that sentence is *still*.

Being single isn't a sign you're defective. It's not evidence against your allure. It's not anything but a state of being, not unlike being hungry or cold.

You're single because you just are. Full stop.

Do your best to not let others' projections infiltrate your outlook of yourself or your love life. Don't allow someone else's wondering why you're solo make you feel pressured to rush into a relationship just to say you're in one.

Instead, when your aunt innocuously asks you where your S.O. might be at Thanksgiving dinner, say something like: "They're not here at the moment, but I can't wait to introduce you to them when I finally meet them. Will you pass the cheesy potatoes, please?"

You just haven't met them yet. You're doing you. And if anyone makes you feel bad about it, that's their own insecurity.

Answer the Dreaded Question in an Empowered Way

In the space here, answer the "dreaded question" in an empowered way. Think about other things you're working toward other than an S.O. List those things here, and be prepared to answer the dreaded question with what is important besides falling in love.

_____

_____

_____

_____

_____

_____

_____

_____

_____

_____

_____

_____

_____

_____

_____

_____

_____

_____

ALONE, NOT LONELY; LONELY, NOT ALONE

A comforting truth: *Alone* doesn't mean "lonely," just as *single* doesn't mean "unwanted." It's just a state of being.

Think of all the ways you spend time with yourself. Think about ways you can pursue your career, your hobbies, your passions. Think about everything you can do, partnered or not.

And, to be honest, there might be a time after you do fall in love that you miss those solo nights in your apartment. When the dishes in the sink were only yours. When someone else's alarm clock didn't wake you up an hour earlier than *you* had to wake up. When you got to watch whatever you wanted on *Netflix*, no questions asked. Yes, companionship is wonderful. But it's okay to enjoy your own company too. In fact, it's necessary.

If you're still not convinced, that's okay. This is absolutely a difficult mindset shift to get down but worth mastering. Even though there are times you will *feel* lonely, it doesn't mean you are alone. You have friends. Family. Maybe a doggo you're nuts about. And you have yourself. Yes, you always have you, right?

You can be alone and not lonely. You can be lonely but not alone. You can embrace all of these moments, and you should.

List Why You're Grateful to Be Single RN

There's a lot to be grateful about when you're single and so much to embrace while you are. Here are some examples to get you started. I appreciate I can:

★ Take up as much room as I want in my bed

★ Only consider myself when making Friday night plans

★ Fully control the aux cord in my car

★ _____

★ _____

★ _____

★ _____

★ _____

★ _____

★ _____

★ _____

★ _____

★ _____

★ _____

★ _____

★ _____

★ _____

★ _____

★ _____

WHEN LOVE IS RUNNING LATE, DOUBLE-CHECK THE TIME

If you think you're too late for love, have you considered that it's because you're a little early? That maybe it's not the right timing just yet, at least for you?

Time lines are complete and utter bullshit. Yep, it's true. This applies to finding love as well. Just because your friends found love doesn't mean you won't one day too.

Okay, so you're not in love right now. Maybe you've had your heart snatched from your chest only to get it back in pieces. And yet, you still found a way to put it back together on your own. Or perhaps you've been super busy building your own goddamn empire. Whatever the case, this is *your* story. Have a little faith in it. Be hopeful for what's to come.

You're exactly where you're meant to be. Every decision you've made, everything you didn't want to happen that did, every reroute you've had to take in order to keep moving is the reason you've arrived where you are. You should be proud.

We start at different places, so how could we take the same route? If you're still grappling with why you're single, look backward. Consider the events, big and small, that led you to the present moment. If you do that, you'll understand it all makes perfect sense.

Love isn't late. It's just running its course. It'll happen, all in good time.

Check Your Timing

Everything that has occurred up to this moment has contributed to where you are now. You can't catch the train at 10 a.m. if you wake up at 9:48 a.m. and live twenty minutes away! I'm not saying you can plan for love, but you can understand why it hasn't worked out. You haven't met the right person yet. In the following space, write out some experiences that have led up to this moment.

YOU'RE THE MAIN CHARACTER

In case you needed a reminder: You're the main character of your life. This is your stage; it's not a dress rehearsal, and it sure as hell isn't a practice run. This is your show. You're the director, producer, *and* star. Take ownership of every part of it.

If you don't feel like your main character, why? Why do you keep stepping out of your own light? Why are you hiding backstage? Why are you giving other people your lines? Why are you letting others write your script?

Is it fear? Lack of confidence? Self-esteem issues? Whatever it may be, you need to face it. You don't want to wake up one day and realize you lived someone else's life, or worse, you lived only for the approval of other people. What a tragedy that would be, eh?

Often when we're single and thinking about pursuing love, we get hyperfocused on the other person we're trying to date. We think of all the ways we can become something they'll like. We time our texts to coordinate with what we think they will appreciate. This is not main character behavior. It puts the power in their hands instead of our own. It puts the spotlight on them instead of on you.

What do *you* want? What could they do to win *you* over?

You're not a supporting role. You're the main attraction. Don't forget that.

Flip the Script

Think about some ways you might be acting like a side character in your own story. When is the last time you put yourself first? When was the last time you considered your needs? When is the last time you felt so goddamn alive you couldn't believe you got to exist at all? Write about it here.

ACTUALLY, NO, YOU *DON'T* NEED TO LOVE YOURSELF FIRST

Self-love doesn't come easy to me. Besides math, it is probably the thing I struggle with most. If you told me to say self-love affirmations in the mirror every morning, I would be as likely to succeed at that as I would at figuring out what the value of x is so I can finally tell my Algebra 2 teacher, Ms. C., what time she needs to get to the train station.

When someone advises me to love myself before someone else does, I want to scream. If I have to do that, I will 100 percent die alone—and I'd prefer not to. If you also struggle with self-love, you've probably heard this advice too. While it's well meaning, it is more damaging than it is helpful. It's also not true.

Self-love is a practice. It's not some oasis you arrive and then *bam!* Self-love!

Being human will get in the way of self-love. You'll have off days. You're going to get frustrated. What matters in these moments is how you reroute from being your own worst enemy to a friend.

If you've decided not to date because you think you're not self-loving *enough*, even though you're trying every single day, you might want to rethink that decision. The right person for you won't impede the self-love process; they'll just give you company along the way. They will cheer you on and provide feedback. You are still your own person, with a partner or not. If you want to start dating, do it. Even if you don't love yourself first.

List Ways You'll Practice More Self-Love Daily

You don't need to love yourself first, but as previously mentioned, it *at least* needs to be on the agenda. In this space, list some self-care practices you will try to implement into your everyday life. For example: *I will fill my own cup before pouring out to others.*

★ _____
★ _____
★ _____
★ _____
★ _____
★ _____
★ _____
★ _____
★ _____
★ _____
★ _____
★ _____
★ _____
★ _____
★ _____
★ _____
★ _____
★ _____

ROMANTICIZE YOUR LIFE

If you're not currently falling in love with another human being, may I recommend falling in love with your life instead?

There is so much wonder and beauty to be felt while you're here. Sure, finding a soul mate is one of those things. But there are so many corners of the earth to explore, so many *nonromantic* soul mates to encounter, so much to learn about yourself, about others, about life.

You need to romanticize your life if you want to fall in love with it. You need to feel lucky you looked out the window at the very moment the clouds blushed pink at sunset. You need to feel gratitude for existing at the same time as Lizzo. You need to give yourself permission to be sad when you are, because this is part of a full human experience, and it means you're alive. You need to dote on your friends. You need to chase your curiosity as if your life depends on it.

Get dressed up for your weekly Target run. Take yourself on the date you wish you could go on. Purchase concert tickets to your favorite band's upcoming show. Reread your favorite book to absorb as much of it as you can while you're existing. Have champagne on a Wednesday. Let the little things matter too much. Take up space, and don't apologize for laughing loudly.

Live in such a way that you look back at your one life with love, not regret.

List Ways You'll Fall in Love with Existing

What makes your heart burst with excitement? What would you be damn pissed you missed? I, for one, will be upset if I never get a chance to take myself on a pasta tour of Italy or pull together my dream home, doing the hard work myself. On this page, list experiences you want to have and how they will make you feel enchanted by your life.

★ _____

★ _____

★ _____

★ _____

★ _____

★ _____

★ _____

★ _____

★ _____

WHO ARE YOU OUTSIDE OF SOMEONE ELSE?

The absence (or presence) of a relationship doesn't define you. Sure, it could be a way you describe yourself, but it's hardly the most interesting thing about you. There is so much more to a person than who they are or aren't dating. Whether someone is engaged or married is less interesting, at least to me, than hearing about what someone is passionate about. What makes them laugh. Their favorite band. What age they were when everything went wrong. (Just kidding!)

The thing is that there are so many ways we can define ourselves. I, for one, identify myself as a pasta enthusiast, a Capricorn, and a golden retriever in a past life, with a lifelong passion for giving unsolicited advice (so writing this book is a dream come true). I am also kind. Loving. Someone who tries to do the right thing, even after getting it wrong. I don't quit. I keep going. I am resilient.

There is so much about me that has nothing to do with anyone else, romantic or otherwise. But let's stay focused on the romantic sense. You are a catch, even if you haven't been caught yet. You are worthy of love. You are interesting, even if someone else isn't sleeping beside you. You are enough as you are, even if you haven't found someone else to love yet.

No one else defines you but you, your character, and your willingness to grow. Never forget that.

Define Yourself Outside of a Relationship Status

What are some ways you can define yourself *outside* of a romantic relationship status? Who are you, really? What makes you tick? What do you do for work? Do you prefer experiences or gifts? What makes you cry? Who would you call right now if you could? What is your favorite memory? What would you do if you won the lottery? You are someone outside of romance. Remind yourself of that on this page.

YOU ARE WHOLE ON YOUR OWN

You don't need anyone else to complete you. You are whole on your own. You always were and always will be. But when you're chronically unchill, this can be easy to forget. After all, when it comes to dating, you might be chasing validation found in the form of another person. It's as if someone else feeling the same way you do is proof of your worth. The final piece you've been needing to be complete.

It's understandable you might feel this way. When you've been told so often that you're too much, the idea of someone else finally seeing your overflow as what they want and need feels like an exhale. It's as if you can finally look in the mirror and see someone looking back who is worthwhile. When this happens, you think, "I will finally feel okay as I am."

You need to know that this isn't a mindset to live by. Like, at all. It's incorrect at its best, and dangerous at its worst. You need to get rid of the idea that another person makes you someone of value, because it's simply not true.

You were someone before them. You have your own history. You've learned, you've lost, you've loved. You've been disappointed, you've been delighted, you've made mistakes. You have friends, a family. All of this happened before you even learned this other person's name. Simply being alive is evidence that you are whole. A significant other entering your atmosphere should add to your world, not become it.

Paint the Whole Picture

To help you start cultivating the mindset that you are whole on your own, write out everything that makes you who you are outside of a romantic relationship. Here are some examples:

★ I am a friend.

★ I am a hard worker.

★ I am an animal lover.

★ _____

★ _____

★ _____

★ _____

★ _____

★ _____

★ _____

★ _____

★ _____

★ _____

★ _____

★ _____

★ _____

★ _____

★ _____

★ _____

THERAPIST-APPROVED SELF-LOVE ACTIVITIES

Self-love is a practice. It's something you must work at daily. It looks different to everyone, but in general, self-love is self-care. It's filling your own cup. It's accepting when something is no longer serving you and rerouting. There are a number of ways to practice self-love daily, and the following ideas are therapist-approved:

★ Take yourself to dinner
★ Get manis and pedis, if that's your thing
★ Write yourself love letters
★ Buy yourself flowers
★ Take yourself on the date you wish someone else would
★ Adopt a skincare routine
★ Journal
★ Watch your favorite romantic comedy
★ Get your hair cut
★ Exercise in a way that works for you and your body
★ Go on a long walk
★ Nourish your body with a healthy meal
★ Treat your mind with your favorite food (even if it's "unhealthy")

Those are just some ideas to get you started. Highlight the ideas that make sense to you, sound fun, and seem as if they'd serve you well. These are all meant to remind you of who you are, even if no one else is around to appreciate you. You get to appreciate you. You are worth your own love. You are worthy of your own respect.

Plan a Self-Love Weekend

Besides the daily self-love tasks just listed, sometimes it might be helpful to dedicate one full weekend entirely to self-love and self-care. You can do this as often as once a month or break it into every quarter. Whatever works for you. Plan out your ideal self-love weekend here.

YOU'RE YOUR OWN CONSTANT

You are your own constant. You go to bed with yourself; you wake up with yourself. You are your own responsibility. Your happiness is in your own hands. Your healing is up to you. Your life and what you do with it is up to you too.

This might sound a little scary, but I promise you, it's not. In fact, it's empowering as *hell*. You're the most consistent person in your life. You are capable of giving yourself everything you ever needed. You don't have to wait around for someone else to do something for you; you can do it for your own damn self, TYSM!

You deserve your own love. You are worthy of your own care. You need to keep this in your mind always.

You are your own constant. Behave accordingly.

The next time you're feeling a little sad about being solo, remember you're not alone. You always have you. You always can depend on yourself. If no one is choosing you, choose yourself this time. Commit to yourself. Come home to yourself. Love yourself.

Share How You'll Commit to Yourself

In this exercise, you're going to write affirmations circulating around the idea of being your own constant. Recite these when you're feeling lonely, when you feel as if you've got no one by your side. I got news for you: You've got *you*. Embrace your own heart.

♥ INTENTIONAL SINGLENESS

What is intentional singleness? Glad you asked! Intentional singleness is being purposeful with your time spent solo. It's enjoying your own company. It's understanding what kind of person will actually be worth changing your status from "Single" to "In a Relationship" on *Facebook* (JK, no one does that anymore). As the name suggests, it's all about intention.

When you're intentional with your time, your heart, and your life, it makes a big difference. You'll find that things will start to fall into place. You will feel at peace with yourself. You will invite a sense of calm, despite any of life's storms. Everything will begin to feel lighter but also weightier and full of meaning. Being intentional is taking control of what you can control and letting go of the rest. After all, you know that was never up to you in the end anyway.

When it comes to intentionality and singleness, think about what you get to do with only being responsible for you. That's what freedom is made of. It's using your time wisely; it's choosing what energy you let into your life and what you show the door. It's practicing conscious decisions whenever you're able to.

Start each day with intention. Write out your intentions if necessary to keep you on track. Journal about how you made it work or what you still need to work on to be more present.

Don't be a bystander in your own life. Be intentional. Live it fully.

Write Your Intentional Singleness Manifesto

Write your Intentional Singleness manifesto. Don't be afraid to make it damn epic. Think of all the ways you'll make your single life *kick-ass* and your own. You'll find love when you least expect it. So might as well enjoy your life now too.

READ THIS WHEN EVERYONE IS GETTING MARRIED

I was waiting for the water to boil for my Kraft Macaroni & Cheese when I saw another engagement announcement pop up on *Instagram*. While I was totally happy for the couple, I also just felt sad. I started to worry love wasn't going to happen for me. Shouldn't it have happened already?

If you're single and have ever scrolled through social media, you've probably felt this way at some point too. It's a shitty feeling. But it's also just that—a feeling. These are not facts. These don't represent reality.

You haven't failed because you haven't found love by twenty-nine or thirty-two or forty and beyond. It's just proof you have standards. You know what you're worth. You refuse to be with someone for the sake of saying you're in a relationship because society seems to think you should be.

Focus on finding true connection, not racing to some imaginary finish line. Sure, this might mean you're solo a bit longer, but it's *always* better to be alone than with the wrong person.

The next time you're comparing your singledom to someone's engagement or wedding post, take a step back. Remember everyone has a different story. How boring would it be if we all followed the same path anyway? Like the post, and take a break from your phone. Give yourself time to process what it is you're feeling, and once you do? Let it go. And then, enjoy your mac 'n' cheese. It's getting cold.

List Things to Look Forward to Other Than Your Wedding

Don't get me wrong. Weddings are a damn good time as a guest, so being the main event is probably even more fun, especially when it's shared with your damn soul mate. But there are tons of other events and experiences to look forward to. Use the space here to list some.

Chapter 3

PUTTING YOURSELF OUT THERE

How to Navigate First Dates, the Talking Stage, and Ghosting with Confidence

Modern dating is tough. But there are some ways to make it a little easier and navigate the scene with a little more confidence, self-respect, and sanity. That's what this chapter is for. You'll notice this is the longest chapter. This is because dating takes a lot of time. You don't find your person immediately, in most cases, especially now. That's okay. Enjoy the ride.

CULTIVATE AN AUTHENTIC DATING STYLE

It's important to keep in mind that one person's dating life will always look different than someone else's. As well, what you want at one time might look different later. You might decide you just want to date casually for a while after a nasty breakup. Or you're finally ready to seek out the real deal. Self-awareness and honesty are key in determining what kind of dating life makes sense for you.

As well, keep in mind your journey is not linear. This is okay, normal, and to be expected. Ultimately, what makes sense for you will make sense for the right person for you.

Stay true to yourself. You don't have to be someone else in order to find love. That never works.

Check in with yourself often. Ask yourself how you're feeling, what you're struggling with, who you've vibed with and didn't. Consider what's going right and which parts of your dating life need more attention. For example, you may feel insecure after getting ghosted, and the fear of it happening again is affecting every date since. In this scenario, remind yourself ghosting says everything about the ghost and not the ghosted. It's cowardly and lazy, a sign of emotional immaturity. You could get ghosted again, but you also might fall in love. The person at drinks now isn't the person who left you on "Read" last month.

Be authentic, behave according to your values, ask for what you need. Love will fall into place one day if you do that.

Build a Dating Life That Makes Sense for You

In the following space, start imagining what you want your life to look like. What kind of partner are you seeking? Are you looking for something serious? Casual? Slow? Ready to hit the ground running? Brainstorm your answers here.

HOW TO NOT OVERTHINK YOUR WAY INTO CANCELING

One of my best friends almost canceled on her first date with her now doting, loving S.O. Why, you ask? Because she overthought everything leading up to the moment she stepped into the bar. She didn't see the point in going because she thought she'd end up disappointed in the end, either by not liking him or him not liking her.

Most people have been there. Sometimes, you might cancel before even giving love a chance because it's a way to protect yourself. After all, you can't be rejected if you never show up to try. You can't be disappointed if you didn't get your hopes up in the first place. You can't feel pain if you never took the L.

Unless you're getting weird vibes from someone who makes you feel unsafe, always go on the date if you're into it. Stop letting fear hold you back. Stop allowing what could go wrong prevent something from going so very right.

Worst case, they're just a dinner date. You can still enjoy the outing. Or, if it's a total bust, you still got practice going on a date. You got practice learning how to tolerate someone for a quick beer. You get practice letting someone know you're not feeling it.

It's just a date. Keep that in mind, and let those shoulders relax a bit.

You got this.

Contemplate Why You Want to Cancel

In the space here, think about why you're feeling the need to cancel. Is it because the person is making you feel unsafe? By all means, cancel. But if it's fear of not feeling good enough or worrying that you'll just end up disappointed? Well, maybe not the best call. Figure it all out here, and go from there (or not).

♥ STUDY THESE FIRST DATE TIPS

While everyone is different in their dating styles and what they want at a particular moment in their life, there are some universal experiences when it comes to first dates, one being *hella* nerves. Most people are going feel a little apprehension before a first date. That's totally normal, BTW, but it can be helpful to calm yourself down a bit. Some ways to do this include:

★ Instead of asking yourself what could go wrong, ask yourself what could go *right*

★ Listen to a pump-up playlist (see the section If Confidence Was a Song, Which One Would It Be? for more on this)

★ Remember, you're there to connect, not convince

★ Acknowledge your nerves, and then remind yourself all is well; it's just a date, not a trial of your self-worth

★ Listen to your instincts

★ Be curious, above all else

★ Call a friend before to remind you of the badass you are

★ Read *Reddit* threads about first dates to feel less alone in your jitters

Ultimately, you're probably always going to feel a little nervous before meeting up with someone new. That's okay. Don't let the fear control your behavior. Rather, let it be your hope.

Give Yourself a Pep Talk

In the following space, compose a pep talk to read to yourself before first dates. Employ some of the first date tips on the previous page, but also give yourself your own damn advice. You know yourself best, after all. You know more than you think you do; you know the answers. Show off that knowledge here.

MAKE YOUR OWN DATING RULES

Screw the game. Make your own damn dating rules.

But what does that mean exactly?

It means taking control of your love life. It means owning what you want. It means respecting yourself. It means setting boundaries with others and with yourself. For example: "I will not tolerate disrespect."

Basically, it's creating your own standards. It's refusing to mess with others' heads and refusing to let others mess with your heart.

It's not carefully timing your texts to seem super MySterIouS. It's responding when you have time. It's making the first move, even if it's uncomfortable. It's letting someone know you like them when it's appropriate and not waiting until you are completely up in your head about it.

It's time to throw away the old rules. It's not working, and the world is different now. Forget waiting three days to call. Forget playing hard to get. Forget acting too busy to care. Forget being aloof. Forget forcing someone to try to read your mind.

Speak up. Show up. Be present. It'll get you further than leaving someone on "Read" for six hours.

Write Your Modern Dating Playbook

In this exercise, you're going to write your own modern dating play-book. Write what you will and won't tolerate. Think about what would be against your "rules," aka your boundaries. Think about what helps someone win your heart and what helps someone lose you. Consider foul plays, skillful dating practices, and more.

IF CONFIDENCE WAS A SONG, WHICH ONE WOULD IT BE?

Psychology has shown us that music can either lift our mood or re-inforce it, based on whatever it is we're listening to. So, keeping this in mind, perhaps creating a self-confidence playlist could be a fantastic route for cultivating some.

Use Spotify or Apple Music or even *YouTube* to create a getting-ready playlist curated specifically for dates. Think about the songs that make you feel like the most badass version of yourself, that inspire confidence, that make you feel *good*. When in doubt, Lizzo and Ariana Grande are some solid go-to artists for finding empowering jams that are also upbeat as hell.

You need to cultivate confidence before a date because you *deserve* to feel confident. You deserve to be putting your best foot forward in this type of situation—and to show off whatcha got! You are worthy; you are wonderful; you have so much to offer. Sometimes, we just need to spark the mood.

Soon enough, you'll be feeling "Good As Hell."

Skip the sad songs for now. It's time to pump yourself up.

Curate a Getting-Ready Playlist

Brainstorm some ideas for your playlist here. Here are some song suggestions to get you started:

"Good As Hell" by Lizzo
"Truth Hurts" by Lizzo
"thank u, next" by Ariana Grande

❤ HOT IS A MINDSET, AND SO ARE YOU!

Research has shown that the more confident someone appears, the more attractive they seem. Not feeling so confident, though? That's okay, you're still hot; you just need to remind yourself of everything you have going for you.

This goes beyond looks, though. This is really what's skin-deep. Stop focusing so much on what the mirror shows. Rather, focus on what vibe you're giving off. How kind you are. How warm you are. How you always try to do the right thing and try to make up for it when you do get it wrong. How you are a little quirky and that's what makes you interesting.

Basically, own your shit. Be who you are. Accept what you are and embrace a growth mindset. These things all contribute to confidence. But if you need a few more action items, here are some tips.

QUICK DATING CONFIDENCE TIPS

★ Wear an outfit that **1** is flattering, **2** makes you feel most like you, **3** is comfortable AF, and **4** gives you hella confidence.

★ List your accomplishments; think about the cool stuff you've already done, no partner needed, career-based, hobby-focused, whatever you're excited about.

★ Call your BFF and ask them to remind you what they love about you.

★ Write out your positive attributes that have nothing to do with looks.

★ Remember this person doesn't dictate your worth.

★ Keep in mind that dates are about what you want too, not just the other person.

List What You Like about Yourself

In this space, list your favorite attributes, physical and otherwise. Remind yourself who you are and what you have to offer. There's a lot, after all! Like it, and list it.

♥ THROW AWAY YOUR "TYPE"

Sure, having a "type" is normal. But is your type keeping you closed off for the person who's actually right for you?

This isn't about having no standards or general understanding about what you want from another person romantically. But being inflexible about what you want is guaranteed to keep you in a loop, potentially repeating the same dating problems over and over. Dating experts warn while it's fine to look for certain qualities in a partner, becoming rigid about the type of person you'll date can end up boxing you in.

In fact, letting yourself date someone who isn't your usual "type" can actually have a slew of benefits, including greater empathy, a new perspective, a new skill set, maybe even a new partner.

If you realize you continue to date a particular type of person and it keeps not working out, try swiping right on someone you wouldn't normally go for. Then go out with them. See what happens. Who knows? You might find the love of your life, because you allowed yourself to go out with someone who loves country music.

Reflect On a Date with Someone Who Wasn't Your Type

This activity will require you to go on a date with someone who you wouldn't normally go for. After you do, write about your experience in the space provided.

_____

_____

_____

_____

_____

_____

_____

_____

_____

_____

_____

_____

_____

_____

_____

_____

_____

_____

_____

DISRESPECT IS THEIR PROBLEM, NOT YOURS

An important reminder: Disrespect says everything about them and nothing about you.

If someone treats you like crap, that is their issue. Truly. Of course, it's easy to turn to self-blame when someone you're really into hurts you. After all, if you can rationalize it as something you did, you can either **A** fix it or **B** feel a sense of control in future scenarios. For example:

> If only I hadn't sent that text so soon, maybe they'd still be into me since I'd have seemed more mysterious and less desperate.
>
> Maybe if I settled for being FWB like they wanted, they wouldn't be ghosting me.
>
> Damn, I wish I hadn't shown any interest. I bet they'd still want to hang out with me today.

Consider this: Their behavior is just that, theirs. It is a reflection of their inner world. Nothing you say or do can change what they did or what they will do. That's okay, because you know what? Your behavior is your own too. You can adjust your boundaries. You can revoke their access to you. You get to decide what you allow and what you don't.

You have the right to stick up for yourself. You're not overreacting by letting someone know when they've crossed a line. You're not "sensitive" or asking for too much. But if you share your truth and you're met with pushback? Then you're asking the wrong person. Let them go.

Swipe left on disrespect. Choose kindness and care. You deserve that much (and more).

Swipe Left on These Disrespectful Behaviors

Write out some behaviors that you flat out refuse to tolerate from a romantic interest. Once you identify them, brainstorm ways you will address 'em. I'll go first:

> I refuse to be blown off without an explanation.
> If a guy and I have plans and he never follows through, I will talk to him about it after a few days when I've cooled off and let him know it wasn't cool. Then, based on his reaction, I will either move on or move forward.

Now it's your turn.

_____

_____

_____

_____

_____

_____

_____

_____

_____

_____

_____

_____

SOME PEOPLE ARE JUST A DINNER DATE, AND THAT'S OKAY

Some people are just in your life for an evening. And that's okay.

Seriously, it really is *okay*. And here's why:

Sometimes, a date is just a date. Sometimes, even if you have fun, you only get to enjoy someone for an evening. But there is still something to be valued from these types of experiences. You can walk away with a new perspective on life. A laugh. A great time. A damn good meal. A new favorite drink. New music recommendations. Maybe even some more confidence.

After all, the more dates you go on, the more practice you get. You'll have more opportunities to start getting through those first date nerves. (Exposure therapy?) You'll learn to navigate those choppy small-talk waters at the start of an evening with more grace. You'll come to recognize when you truly aren't feeling it and how to end the outing in a kind, not terribly awkward way.

You really can't go wrong most times by going on a date. Just because someone isn't made for longevity doesn't mean they don't teach you something. It doesn't mean you can't enjoy them for what they were, when they were.

Appreciate the outing. Thank them for their company. Wish them well. Go your separate ways. Be glad you went.

Some people will only be a dinner date. And that's more than enough sometimes.

List What You Take with You

List things you can get out of a single date. Get creative and draw from past experiences too. Maybe someone pointed you in the direction of a great place to stargaze. Or made you laugh your ass off, even though you didn't feel that romantic vibe. Whatever it is, list it here:

★ _____

★ _____

★ _____

★ _____

★ _____

★ _____

★ _____

★ _____

★ _____

DON'T SWEAT THE SMALL STUFF

I am a bit of a hot mess sometimes. Unfortunately, this side of me doesn't always get hidden on dates. You'd think I'd learn to master allure, a hint of mystery. Not oversharing every little detail about my life. But no. I say too much, then get home and lie in my bed wondering why I told him about that stupid thing I did in 2007—and now only he and I know about because every other normal person who witnessed the event has forgotten about it.

I'm spiraling. Lemme take a second.

Okay, we back.

Basically, nothing you do is as embarrassing as you may think. No one is thinking about you as much as you're thinking about you; the truth is, they're thinking about themselves. What a relief, eh? This is not to say be a complete weirdo since it'll be forgotten. It just means don't worry so much if you think you say or do something a little awkward.

Don't sweat the small stuff. It's not worth it.

Fuh-get about It!

In this exercise, reflect on some dates you've been on, and think back to those things you said or did that have been haunting you ever since. Once you do, cross 'em out. Let it go. No one cares or remembers. Yay!

♥ IN DEFENSE OF NO CHILL

One way people hope to snag their dream date is by acting super, super, super chill. Ice-cold. No problems, no worries. Just smooth sailing. Needs? Who has those? Standards? Psh. If you're the human version of a succulent plant, then this probably indeed does work well for you. But since you're reading this book, I'm guessing not.

And yet we still try. We try to be chill by staying silent. Going with the flow. Acting #natural. Because somewhere along the way, we learned speaking up for what we want makes us demanding. That wanting something serious makes us crazy. That having standards makes us stuck up.

And you know what? Screw that!

Because the truth is this: If you have needs and fail to express them, they aren't going to be met. Eventually, these unmet needs will turn into resentment and make themselves known in one way or another. It's not fair to the people you date or yourself to not speak up for what it is you need and want out of the relationship.

Instead, be completely unchill. If you like someone, tell them. If you want to make it *Facebook*-official, tell them. If you didn't like the way they treated you, *tell them*. Because you have nothing to lose if you have nothing to gain, right? Speak up. Be notoriously unchill. Eventually, you'll find someone just as off the rails as you. And you'll be thankful they weren't afraid to let their crazy show. (Just don't be scary and aggressive, that's different.)

Defend Your Lack of Chill

In the space here, write out why it's okay to care a little too much and be a little too there. This is not to say it's okay to cross boundaries or be an actual psycho, but that you're allowed to own what you want and what you need.

SIGNS YOU'RE OVERTHINKING AGAIN, AND HOW TO STOP

Overthinking—it's kind of the worst. For some of us, it's particularly grueling when it comes to finding an S.O. Given that you picked up this book, I'm going to make an assumption that you're one of these folks. Same. Luckily, there are some pretty telltale signs that you're overthinking (and how to stop). For example:

> You're projecting old pain on a new situation.
>
> You are feeling totally frantic.
>
> You're focusing on the feelings, not the facts.
>
> You're meddling in the *what-ifs.*
>
> You're replaying something that's already happened over and over and over and over again.

These are typical signs you're overthinking something. Here are some general points for when you're spiraling:

> You can't control what's already happened. Damage control, in most cases, is a myth.
>
> Remember other people get nervous too.
>
> Most of the time, things aren't as personal as they feel.
>
> Everyone has pain you'll never know about.
>
> History won't always repeat itself.

Overthinking happens to the best of us, and it's easy to do in situations in which we feel vulnerable, like dating. However, it can totally derail what could be a fun experience. Learning to recognize when you're overthinking versus actually assessing a situation will be helpful in learning how to stop and reroute.

Give Yourself a Designated Worry Time

Set a timer for ten minutes. While the clock is running, spiral in the space provided. Once the timer is up, put your pencil down. Stop writing. Turn the page. Signify that the spiral is over.

❤ ADDRESS THE RED FLAGS

There are some definite red flags to look out for in a relationship. According to Healthline.com, controlling behaviors, disrespect for boundaries, not enough time together, unequal feelings, and unkind communication are all sure signs a relationship or situationship is unhealthy and not likely to last.

Some things, such as communicating boundaries or sticking up for yourself, can be worked on. There is certain behavior you should absolutely, 100 percent never fucking tolerate, including any type of abuse.

And if someone you're dating apologizes for bad behavior but then continues to do said bad behavior, that's not good enough. Sorry without change is merely manipulation. That's not someone you want in your life, let alone someone to date.

Red flags can be difficult to address, but in the end, identifying them will save you a lot of pain and long-term agony. Recognizing signs early on that someone might not be a good fit for you is important. Be honest, direct, and brave enough to walk away when it's time.

Have your own back. Don't tolerate less than what you deserve.

Prepare to Address the Red Flags

If you want to give someone a chance to change their behavior, go for it. Draft what you might say here.

_____

_____

_____

_____

_____

_____

_____

_____

_____

_____

_____

_____

_____

_____

_____

_____

_____

_____

_____

_____

_____

_____

ARE YOU ATTRACTING OR CHASING?

Manifestation is a self-help practice that relies on the Law of Attraction. It basically says that what we put out into the universe, we get back. I used to think it was bullshit. However, I can now see how this is more of a change in energy and mindset than actually being able to control the outcomes.

Energy is everything. The vibrations we feel are no accident. You know how sometimes you just have a "bad feeling" about someone and end up being right? That's energy, baby! Notice it, and listen to it.

It's important to ask yourself if you're attracting the right person or chasing all the wrong people when dating. If you're constantly being the one to reach out, if you feel as if they're more work than they are wonderful, if you are constantly losing your breath, then you might be chasing someone who has zero intention of ever being caught (at least by you).

I know that sucks, but it's also good to realize when this is the case. Because you don't want someone who doesn't want you. End of story.

Don't chase someone. Attract them. This will always feel safer and calmer. Feelings of chaos and stress indicate chasing. Stop that.

So, in short, be the energy you want in your life. You get what you give. What goes around, comes around. Embrace the karma. It's always in your favor.

Determine Whether You're Attracting or Chasing

Use this space to create a chart. Label one column "Attracting." Write out some ways you attract the love you want. Label the second column "Chasing." In that column, write down all the ways you chase love. Here are some ideas to get you started: I attract love when I share my needs. I chase love when I stay quiet after someone disrespects me.

SO, YOU'VE REACHED THE "TALKING STAGE"

The talking stage can truly be the absolute *worst*. Because it's deeper than friendship. But it's not romantic—yet—but it could be? Maybe? But what if they're just being friendly? What if it *is* just friendship?

Lines are blurry in the talking stage. It can be more frustrating than a situationship. There is so much gray area. It's a lot of going with the flow and feeling it out, or at least it's best when it's approached in this manner. However, that's wayyyyy easier said than done. At times, the talking stage is what makes or breaks the chance of romance because one party, or both parties, get way too in their heads.

It's easy to stress that your feelings are unknown and you might miss your shot. You might consider a lot of time has passed and this must mean they're not into you. But think about it like this: You're still into them, right? So, it's possible they're just doing what you're doing too.

So you have a few choices:

1 *Keep going with the flow and suffering*
2 *Rush it and suffer*
3 *Let them know how you feel, when the time feels right*

In the end, you have nothing to lose by sharing what you want. You're allowed to want more. You're allowed to be honest about that. And if it does end up being just friendship, then at least you know and can heal and move on. (And have a friend too.)

Navigate the "Talking Stage" with *Minimal* Insanity

Okay, so now that we've covered the talking stage, journal about what your own experience has been with it here. Share your insecurities. Write about what you're enjoying. Jot down everything and anything.

STOP PUTTING UP WITH BS BEHAVIOR

An ancient proverb says, "If Megan Thee Stallion wouldn't put up with it, neither should you." Joke! I just made that up, but it is a motto everyone should live by when looking for love.

Megan preaches confidence and owning what you want and who you are. She has taught everyone that you deserve everything you want, and more. And if someone is playing with your heart, then you can forfeit the game by not playing back.

If you're dating someone and you're starting to wonder if their behavior is toxic or hurtful to you, then it probably is. And if you bring up their transgressions and they act defensive, deny it, or continue to do whatever it is that you told them was hurting you?

Kick 'em to the curb. We know Megan wouldn't take that shit, and neither should you.

You deserve respect. You deserve someone who holds space for you. You deserve kindness. You deserve understanding. You deserve compassion. Stop allowing anything but this.

Don't be afraid to say goodbye to those who aren't good for you. Let go of those who don't know how to love you or who don't *want* to love you. Say goodbye to those who never really bothered to learn who you were at all.

Make Megan proud. Stop putting up with BS behavior.

Write a Resignation Letter from Disrespect

This is your chance to write out your official resignation letter to tolerate disrespect. No two weeks' notice needed; you're done with it. Bye!

WHAT ARE YOUR SEXUAL BOUNDARIES?

Boundaries are everything. Boundaries keep us safe. Boundaries teach others how to care for and love us. Boundaries make way for expectations and important conversations. And, despite what we may have grown up believing, boundaries don't keep us apart. They bring us closer; they are vital for healthy, bountiful relationships (romantic and otherwise).

Of course, our boundaries vary based on *who* it is we're interacting with. For example, some things, like who you hooked up with over the weekend, you'd tell your best friend but probably not your mom. Audience and context matters.

And while every romantic relationship we encounter won't be the same, there will definitely be overlap.

Knowing your sexual boundaries ahead of time can be extremely helpful. It can help you make safe decisions physically, mentally, and emotionally. Maybe you aren't ready for sex until your relationship is defined. That's okay. Or maybe you are down for that but still want to be treated with respect, of course. Good call.

If you feel uncomfortable communicating your sexual boundaries with someone, then this is probably someone you shouldn't be messing with. Communication, especially about sex, is everything. If you feel as if you can't be up-front, then you might want to let them go.

Determine Your Sexual Boundaries

In this space, write out some of your sexual boundaries and your plan to communicate them with future partners. Think about what you're willing to share and not. Understanding whatever your comfort level is at a given time is just fine. Honor your instincts. They are there for a reason.

_____

_____

_____

_____

_____

_____

_____

_____

_____

_____

_____

_____

_____

_____

_____

_____

_____

_____

_____

_____

STOP LOOKING TOO MUCH INTO TEXTS

Overanalyzing texts is common. And it's pretty maladaptive, to be perfectly honest. Why we overanalyze texts, of course, makes total sense. We don't have the context clues of tone, facial expressions, or body language. It's maddening at times, but it doesn't have to be. There are ways to bring yourself back to Earth when you're scrolling through a text thread trying to determine where everything went wrong.

STEP ONE *Take a damn break from the phone. Literally flip it over, put it in another room, place it out of reach. This could be as long as a few hours to as short as fifteen minutes. The timing you need is dependent on you and when you can feel the spiral being short-circuited.*

STEP TWO *Once you're ready, look at the text one more time. Review the context. Acknowledge which part of it is making you freak out.*

STEP THREE *List why what's freaking you out is most likely the result of overanalyzing, not reality.*

STEP FOUR *If there truly is some issue, address it with the other person. It's okay to be vulnerable and ask for clarification.*

When you finally understand that everything is fine, as it always was, take a deep breath, exhale, and then let all the anxiety go. Remember these skills the next time someone says "lol" instead of "LOL." (Not speaking from personal experience. Nope, not me!)

List the Facts about the Text

Whatever text you're currently overanalyzing, whether it's a response you got or a text you sent, I will tell you one thing: *It. Is. Not. Worth. It.* On the lines provided, draft what's freaking you out, why it's bothering you, and how you're going to either address it or move forward. Then let it go.

♥ SEND THE DAMN TEXT, OMG

So you have a crush. Congrats! Those can be so fun. There's hope, potential, butterflies, excitement. And usually, more often than not, texting.

Texting can be a nightmare when you're an overthinker. After all, there are no visual cues, no tone, nothing to decipher but emojis, shorthand, and context.

What's even more scary is trying to flirt via text. Like, it's actually the worst if you are an overthinker. But it doesn't have to be. In fact, it can be kinda fun, if you let it be.

Think about what the text you're sending is trying to accomplish. Also, feel free to run a draft by your BFF to get another take. It's okay to have a second set of eyes on what you wanna say.

Be confident. Be flirty. Be you. This is all to say:

Send the risky text, ask them out, tell them how you feel, wear the crop top, eat the damn pizza. We're all gonna die one day, so who cares? And if they don't appreciate the sass? Well, on to the next. They didn't deserve your flirting anyway.

Draft the Risky Text

Draft the risky text you're thinking about sending. Think about why you want to send it, what you're trying to achieve, and then... *send it*.

IT'S OKAY TO HAVE STANDARDS

It's time to be honest with yourself: What kind of person are you truly looking for? What are your standards? Who has met your standards in the past? Who hasn't, and why?

You're not stuck up for having standards and nonnegotiables for a date. If anyone says you're being too picky, thank them for their input and stick to your guns anyway.

The truth is, you know what you need and what you desire. Why settle for less than that? You get one life, so you might as well love who you actually enjoy loving.

If someone pushes back against your standards, this is a red flag. Know that you can show them the door. Good riddance!

Please be brave enough to be alone, rather than settling for someone who treats you like shit or isn't on the same page or, frankly, is a bad fit for you. It's truly better to be alone a little longer than with the wrong person.

Love is out there. It's just not here right now. Have faith it'll call back.

Ask Yourself These Questions When Looking for a Partner

When we begin the process of dating, it's sometimes difficult to know exactly what we want. We often think of all the ways we can bend to be who the other person wants, but what about what *we* want? Because that matters too. The following questions might help guide you. You deserve what you want. Don't forget that.

Are they dependable?

_____

_____

Do they listen?

_____

_____

Do they hold space for me?

_____

_____

Do they make me happy?

_____

_____

Do they respect me?

_____

_____

Do they have their own interests?

_____

_____

What are their values?

_____

_____

What are my values?

_____

_____

Do our values clash or align?

_____

_____

Do I like them? Why?

_____

_____

THEY'RE JUST A PERSON, NOT A JUDGE

I used to walk into dates wondering what the person I was going out with would see in me. All I could think about was everything I didn't like about myself. My past. My uncanny ability to overshare before we even ordered the first beer. My sincere love of dad jokes. Ya know, just fun and casual things. So, when it didn't work out, I always determined it was something wrong with me and that I wasn't enough—or too much in the wrong places.

However, after growing into myself a little more, I realize I was projecting my insecurities. I have a lot to offer. I'm kind and funny. I'm aggressively supportive. Sure, I'm a little quirky, but the right person won't mind that. Maybe they'd even find it endearing (at least, I'd like to think so). Also, if I had to change any of my quirks in order for some other person to like me, I'd be betraying myself. Hard pass.

Falling in love isn't about someone else validating you. Dating is for connection. It's for hoping the person sitting across from you sees your fault lines and says, "Hey, I have those too; let's work on it together."

If you read this and thought, Same, hopefully this brought you a new mindset. You aren't your insecurities. You are looking for love, and that shows vulnerability, courage, and hope. Those are beautiful things that deserve to be shared. Hell, I'd argue *need* to be shared. The world needs more love, not less.

What Do You Bring to the Table?

So, now, let's put this new mindset to the test. Write in the empty space about what *you* bring to the table. You have a lot to offer, remember. They chose to go out with you, to spend time with you. Think of all that you are outside of this person. You might just be exactly what they're looking for. And if not? Oh well, on to the next!

❤ DON'T LET A GHOST HAUNT YOU

Ghosting is so common in dating now, and it really sucks. It's unexpected, it's painful, and mostly, it's cowardly. But it's also damaging to our sense of trust.

Ghosting is so prevalent, it's easy to start hunting for signs of someone turning into a ghost. When we first talk with someone, for example, we may look for "clues" about whether they're sticking around (or planning to vanish).

None of this is healthy.

Rather than search for hints that they're planning to dip, be in the moment. Check the facts; look to the evidence of your relationship. Yes, they could ghost, but what if they don't? Don't let some shitty person make you distrust someone else who might deserve your trust.

After all, if someone ghosts you, thank them for doing the legwork of leaving. You don't want someone who doesn't want you.

A ghost will only haunt you if you let them. Don't let their leaving color your current situation. It's not the same person.

Write What You Needed to Hear from Your Ghost

In the space here, journal about the way you wish your ghost had said goodbye to you. Or what you wish you could say to them.

Chapter 4

"SO WHAT ARE WE?"

Defining the Relationship and Falling in Love

So you found someone you want to date officially. Yay! After so many ghosts, flakes, and bygone boos, though, this may be difficult to trust at first. It can be hard not to sprint in the other direction or push them away by overthinking everything and anything. This chapter is all about embracing the free fall, finally defining the relationship, and feeling love once again. Yes, it might not work out, but what if it does? Give love a chance; give *yourself* a chance. And give them a chance too.

♥ WHY DO YOU LIKE THEM?

Okay, so you're definitely attracted to them, but what do you actually like about them? Really dig deep and think about everything that makes them who they are.

Beyond physical characteristics, what do you like? What made you fall for them? Why them and not someone else on Hinge?

The more you notice what you like about your partner, the more you'll fall in love and appreciate that you got the chance to love them.

List Their Best Qualities

In the space that follows, write discernible, evidence-driven reasons why you like this person. For example: "I like their eyes" or "They treat me with respect by doing X" or "They call when they say they will."

_____

_____

_____

_____

_____

_____

_____

_____

_____

_____

_____

_____

_____

_____

_____

_____

_____

_____

_____

♥ SIGNS YOU'RE TOTALLY INTO THEM

So, you've surpassed the talking stage. You're starting to think about committing to this person, and you have good reason to believe they're feeling the same way. You're gassing yourself up to have the DTR talk. You're excited, nervous, and, most importantly, you're falling hard.

But then you start to get in your head. You start questioning whether you *really* like them. Whether you pulled feelings out of thin air because you're bored.

It's time to get over your commitment issues and realize you like them. Need more convincing? Here are some signs you're, like, totally into them:

- *Your heart flutters a little when their name pops up on your phone.*
- *You laugh at their jokes, even though they're not that funny.*
- *When thinking about future plans, you take them into account.*
- *You introduced them to your friends because you knew they'd get along.*
- *There are songs that make you think of them.*
- *You trust their opinion and ask for it.*
- *You feel safe with them in a way you don't with others.*
- *You're thinking of them as you read this list and smiling because you're realizing what you feel.*

Congrats, you've got a case of Got It Bad. Enjoy it.

Admit Your Feelings to Yourself

Alright, so, now that you're probably realizing you're very into this particular human, it's time you admit the damn feelings to yourself too. In the space provided, write out what you've been afraid of and what's been holding you back. Think about past experiences that may be coloring your present. Then, write out why this person is different. Share why you like them. And then, share what you hope you two can be.

❤ IF THE SHOE FITS

Would you wear a shoe that was two sizes too big? What about five sizes too small? Probably not, right? Then why would you date someone who doesn't fit with your life, your values, and yourself?

The truth of the matter is that a solid relationship comes down to fit. You need to work with, not against, each other. You shouldn't be constantly fighting and making up only to do it all again the next day. Some level of conflict is totally normal; constant bickering and unhappiness, on the other hand, is not sustainable or healthy.

Love is work, but it should also feel easy. Safe. Calm. Despite what *Netflix* may tell you, a good partnership isn't draining. Rather, it's invigorating. It gives you space to grow on your own, and together. Even if they're a wonderful person, if your energies don't align, they just don't. It's sad, but it may be the truth.

You are not for everyone, remember? And not everyone is for you. So many things come into play when it comes to a solid partnership. Some such elements include:

★ Your personalities
★ Your life goals
★ Your careers
★ Your nonnegotiables
★ Your ability and willingness to grow together

Find someone who fits you, and who you fit with. Be honest about what you both want now, and in the future.

Put Your Pieces Together

Reflect on your relationship. Think about why it was about fit, not about anyone's worth. Write it all out on these puzzle pieces.

IT DOESN'T NEED TO HURT IN ORDER TO FEEL REAL

Here's a PSA: Painful love is not a deeper love. And it's time you unlearn the idea that a relationship needs to hurt in order to feel real.

It doesn't. In fact, it 100 percent shouldn't.

The truth is so many people, myself included, have romanticized—and still romanticize—intense but toxic relationships. We associate intensity with a deeper, more worthy love, but the truth is something with that much torque ultimately loses its spark. It just isn't sustainable long term; it sure as hell isn't healthy either.

You don't have to burn and burn and burn to call something love.

If you have a tendency to believe that feeling chemistry is the same thing as feeling fucking stressed out all the time about the person you're dating, you might want to reconsider if that's actually true. Hint: *It's not.*

It's going to take some hard work, but you are going to need to understand that love isn't calamity. It's not unsafe. It's not stressful. The truth of the matter is someone you're truly meant to be with won't feel like an open wound; they'll feel like coming home.

So, the real question is: Are you ready to head that way? Are you finally ready to welcome love home?

Romanticize Healthy Love

Okay, so, now that we know toxicity sucks, it's time to romanticize healthy love. In the following space, write out some ways that healthy love can still feel exciting. Consider how you don't need chaos, uncertainty, and instability to stay interested.

READ THIS IF YOU'RE AFRAID TO TELL THEM HOW YOU FEEL

Revealing your feelings to someone you've been seeing is scary. This shouldn't stop you from having the conversation, though.

While it's valid to fear being too eager, dating experts encourage being direct and owning what it is you want with them. No, a phone call or text is not the right approach. Make a point to see them in person and say exactly what you feel.

"I like you. I enjoy spending time with you. I want to see if this can turn into something more. Thoughts?"

Of course, timing does matter. While every couple will have different time lines, research shows two to four months is the standard time to establish feelings for each other. However, feel it out. You know the situation best.

They could be feeling the very same way you do. Someone has to take the leap at some point. Why not have it be you?

If they don't feel the same way? That hurts, and I'm so sorry. It is okay, though. You shared your heart, and that's one of the bravest things you can do. You also practiced owning what you want. You get to let go of someone who couldn't be what you needed. In the end, these are *all* good things.

So, tell them how you feel because you deserve to have your feelings known. You deserve to honor what you feel. You deserve to stop living in what-ifs. And who knows? Maybe love is on the other side of fear.

Write Out How You Feel

Having the conversation is nerve-wracking. However, you don't have to do it on the fly. You can prepare ahead of time; in fact, it might be better if you do. On the following lines, write out how you feel and lay out exactly for the other person what you want.

_____

_____

_____

_____

_____

_____

_____

_____

_____

_____

_____

_____

_____

_____

_____

_____

_____

_____

_____

_____

♥ TRUST THE FREE FALL

It's time to let your guard down. They like you too! They are in a relationship with you now, after all. It's time to stop overthinking every little thing. It's time to trust the free fall. It's time to let yourself truly feel. You're safe now.

Let yourself enjoy the moments of falling in love. Allow yourself to be fully present. Stop being in a relationship with one foot out the door. Bring that foot in. Close the door and stay a while; it's cold out there.

Sure, there's a chance it might not work out. Breakups are always possible. However, reminding yourself you'd be okay without them is a good place to start. You have a solid support system, your own interests, your own life, your own existence outside of this person.

But let's not focus on a potential breakup. Focus on the now.

Notice what you like about them. Breathe in hope and exhale doubt. Let yourself fall for once. Plan fun dates. Tell them when they're doing something cute. Kiss them at the supermarket. Learn their coffee order. Ask them about their day. Listen sincerely.

Love can be fun if you trust it. It's time you did.

Enjoy Them Now

Keeping a level head when you finally commit to someone can be tough. There's the honeymoon stage, but then there's a fear of the other shoe dropping. It's time to quiet that now. Here, write out all the ways you're enjoying your person.

INSECURE MOMENTS HAPPEN (HERE'S HOW TO NOT LET 'EM DERAIL YOU)

Plot twist: You're going to have moments of insecurity in your relationship too. No matter how healthy your partnership may be, how validating and loving your S.O. is, or how confident you've become, you're going to have doubts about yourself. You might get jealous. You might struggle to remember why they picked you. You might even have trouble finding one thing you like about your face when you look in the mirror. It sucks, but it happens.

You're human, and you're bound to have these feelings from time to time. Also, as was drilled into your head in Chapter 2, self-love is a practice, and sometimes, we fall short. Sometimes, we need a little help remembering and working through it.

This is where your boo thing comes in.

Your partner is there to support you, remember. While they're not *responsible* for your feelings and cannot take the painful stuff away, they can help you process it and support you. Especially when it comes to feeling jealous or insecure about their feelings for you, your partner should 100 percent be involved or at least aware.

Be brave, sit them down, and open up a conversation (not a confrontation). For example, if they said something that made you feel shaky about yourself, tell them and explain why. Odds are, they didn't even realize what they said would hurt you. Communication is everything. Speak up. Help them help you.

Prepare to Talk to Your S.O.

List exactly what it is you're feeling insecure about. Then, figure out what you can do to work out the insecurity with yourself. Also write out what your partner can do to help ease your worries and put your mind to rest. While your feelings are up to you to manage, you can ask for help from your S.O.; in fact, you should!

COMMUNICATION IS EVERYTHING

When it comes to dating someone seriously, communication is truly everything. You're in it together. You are a team, a partnership, a goddamn glorious romance. As such, you need to keep them in the loop with where you're at mentally, emotionally, physically, financially, and more.

They can't read your mind, nor should you expect them to. Yes, there are personal cues and body language, but the best way to communicate is with your words.

Being clear and direct with your partner is vital to your relationship's health. Don't expect them to read your mind. They can't. Speak up if you don't want to stay in for the fifth weekend in a row. Let them know you want to go on the town. If you don't, they might assume you're cool with watching *The Office* every Friday. Unless you're cool with that, fucking *say something*. Otherwise, don't expect to be heard. What's unspoken can't be heard, or acted on.

Communication goes both ways too. If you're going to expect your partner to listen to you, then you need to be open to hear what they have to say as well (even if it's something you are not particularly thrilled about).

Communication is everything. Saying what you feel, effectively, never made anything worse; it makes everything that much better.

Write Out What Needs to Be Communicated to You

Some things can remain unspoken, of course; communication is body language and personal cues too. However, sometimes, things need to be said explicitly. For example: consent. Here, write out what always needs to be said out loud to you and to your partner. Some examples include if they've done something to hurt your feelings or what they want for dinner.

SAME BOOK, DIFFERENT PAGES

So, you fell in love first. That's okay.

Remember your partner has their own history and hang-ups too. Sometimes, love comes slower to one person than the other. It doesn't mean it's not going to happen. It just means they're moving at a different pace. While this can understandably make you feel insecure, try your best to not let it get to you. Remind yourself that the two of you are reading the same book—you're just a few pages ahead.

It's okay to fall in love first. It's more than okay; it's brave. It might even give your partner the courage to pick up the pace.

Do your best to enjoy your love, even if it's not 100 percent reciprocated yet. Be patient and loving toward your partner. Try not to resent them. Ask them how you can help them feel comfortable. Keep faith. Keep moving forward.

They'll catch up. Don't worry.

Just give it time. You'd hope if the roles were reversed, they'd do the same for you, right?

Write about It

If you still feel insecure about saying "I love you" first, journal about it here to process your feelings. Figure out how you can share your vulnerability with your partner without making them feel pressured or rushed.

_____

_____

_____

_____

_____

_____

_____

_____

_____

_____

_____

_____

_____

_____

_____

_____

_____

_____

_____

_____

❤ FIRST FIGHT PROBLEMS

So you've had your first fight. Congratulations! This is where the most growth starts to happen. Most times, it shows you're being real with one another, even if it leads to a disagreement.

Fights and conflict are not always a bad thing. They're a human, natural part of being in a relationship. There's a right way to do it, of course, but fighting with your S.O. isn't always the red flag it's made out to be.

A fight opens the door for more communication. Disagreements invite opportunities for discussions. Conflict makes room for compromise.

What a fight shouldn't bring about is abuse. If this is the case, this is the red flag that you need to get out.

When a fight begins, it's okay to take a minute to cool off and gather your thoughts and feelings. Once you're both feeling more levelheaded, sit down and talk. Remember to come to the conversation with the goal of resolving the issue, not reigniting hurt feelings.

You're a team. A partnership. It'll work out, as long as you put in the work.

Be respectful, kind, and hold space for yourself and for your S.O. Eventually, disagreements won't be so scary. They'll be welcome.

Determine Your Fighting Style

There's a way to fight right. Before or after you and your partner get in a heated conversation, draft some talking points here to make sure that you're fighting from a solution-oriented, compassion-based place.

SIGNS OF A NOURISHING RELATIONSHIP

In the end, you want a relationship that nourishes you. That sustains you. That gives you hope for a better tomorrow. That cheers you on as you save yourself.

That's the kind of loving worth fighting for.

Check out this list of signs that a relationship is nourishing. Compare against your own relationship to see if your partner is supporting you or draining you of your very precious energy:

- ★ They challenge you to be your best self
- ★ They love you in your love language
- ★ They hold space for you
- ★ They listen well
- ★ They fight right
- ★ They don't say cruel things to you
- ★ They're communicative
- ★ They're patient
- ★ They're compassionate
- ★ You *like* them in addition to loving them
- ★ You feel like a team
- ★ You like their family
- ★ You see a future with them
- ★ They share similar values to you
- ★ You have your own interests

List Signs of a Nourishing Relationship

In this space, list your own signs of a nourishing relationship. While there are some universal traits, listed on the previous page, share your own ideas of what would make you feel loved, supported, and safe:

★ _____
★ _____
★ _____
★ _____
★ _____
★ _____
★ _____
★ _____
★ _____
★ _____
★ _____
★ _____
★ _____
★ _____
★ _____
★ _____
★ _____
★ _____
★ _____
★ _____
★ _____

MANAGE YOUR EXPECTATIONS

Love isn't like the movies. In fact, it's pretty much nothing like the movies at all. We expect love to be perfect in order for it to last, but that just isn't true. There are going to be plenty of tough moments, both inside and outside your relationship. Parents die. Grandparents die. Jobs get lost. Money can be tight.

TLDR; shit happens. So, how are you two going to make it through as a team? How are you going to manage your expectations and appreciate that you get someone by your side during the hard parts?

Love won't save you. It won't heal you. It won't take away the hard things in life. But it will make it a little more bearable, easier to tolerate.

Make sure you're looking for something real, not something perfect. Reality is better than a fantasy. You should love a person, not a portrait.

Determine Whether You're Expecting Perfection

In the space here, determine whether you're expecting your relationship to be real or whether you're expecting too much and wanting perfection. Think about why that might be.

THE HONEYMOON STAGE ENDS, BUT LOVE DOESN'T HAVE TO

Here's the thing: Your partner is human. Your relationship is human. *You're* human. And with all of this humanity sprinkled into one unit, you're bound to have imperfection, pain, and some goddamn annoyances too.

You can look at these moments of irritation and disappointment and conflict as warning signs, as indications that your relationship is going to come to a screeching halt because there is no way in *hell* you can live the rest of your life with them snoring every time they drink an IPA, saying LOL out loud, or not changing the toilet paper roll at 2 a.m. They weren't this way in the beginning! Why is this annoying stuff coming out now?

The more time you spend with someone, the more likely these parts of them are to show. These annoyances existed in the beginning of the relationship too; they were probably just a little more toned down.

But here's the thing: Everyone is going to be annoying at some point. Including you. If you had to be perfectly serene, exist free of flaws, and have no irritating features to be loved, we'd all be alone.

Your partner isn't perfect. They're going to piss you off. But think about how you'd miss that snore beside you after a night at the bar or their quirky sense of humor. You need to look at love differently if you want it to grow. You need to embrace the messiness, the imperfections. This is actually the good stuff, in the end.

Feel lucky.

Remember Why You Love Them

In the space provided, remember why you were drawn to your S.O. in the first place. Reflect on what made you fall for them. Remind yourself of all the ways you're so glad their yours, even when life gets in the way.

Chapter 5

BREAKING UP F'ING SUCKS

Handling the Heartbreak of an Official Relationship's End

Breaking up with someone will always be hard. Whether you are still in love with them or not, whether you're doing the breaking up or you're the one being broken up with, it's painful. It brings about feelings of grief. But there are ways to cope. To heal. To move forward. This chapter is meant to guide you through just that.

WHEN YOUR RELATIONSHIP IS TOXIC BEYOND REPAIR

When it's time to leave, it's time to leave. Full stop. It's gonna suck, but you'll know when it's over. Your gut will tell you.

If your person is no longer making you happy and, in fact, is making you *unhappy*, this is the telltale sign your relationship is on its last legs.

It can be hard to let go. It can be difficult to recognize that something is over before someone actually says, "We need to break up."

It's so easy to make excuses for someone's bad behavior; it's even easier to blame ourselves because that way we can feel a semblance of control over the situation.

But sometimes, good things fall apart. They turn toxic. And you can't keep inhaling the fumes of a relationship's demise.

It's hard, but you know what you need to do. If you're constantly debating breaking up with someone, it's a sign that you probably need to.

Have your friends at the ready, get tissues, and consider taking off work the next day. Have a plan in place so you can feel ready to catch yourself if you fall.

Prepare to Leave Your Toxic Relationship

In the space provided, write all the ways you'll put your toxic relationship behind you. Think about why you're ending it and what baggage you'll need to leave; don't hold back. This is just for you.

ON LETTING GO OF SOMEONE YOU STILL LOVE

Breakups don't have to be brought about by toxicity. The other person can be wonderful and doting, and you can feel completely suffocated and unhappy too. If they're the wrong person, they're the wrong person; there's nothing you can do about it.

You can love someone and no longer be in love with them. And it's painful, but you need to let them go, for your sake and theirs.

In one way or another, your needs aren't being met in the way you need them to be. Whether their schedule is too busy, they're too jealous of your friends, or whatever, there are some things that can't be worked through.

The only choice left is to say goodbye.

Even if the breakup is the right thing and what you want, it doesn't mean it won't hurt. You can still love people you are no longer *in* love with. It's so painful to hurt someone you care about. But in the end, the most loving thing you can do is set them and yourself free.

Have the talk in person; let them say what they need to say too. It's a two-way street, and they deserve to be heard. Then go your separate ways.

In the days that follow, prepare to ache. Listen to that hurt the way you would a good friend. It's telling you what needs healing. Tend to those spots gently. Wipe away the tears. Brush off the dust. This is how you let go of someone you still love.

Prepare to Break Up with Someone You Still Love

In the space here, plan out how you're going to let go of the person you love but are no longer in love with. Think about exactly what you want to say, what you would like to hear from them, and what you'll need in the weeks that follow to heal.

_____

_____

_____

_____

_____

_____

_____

_____

_____

_____

_____

_____

_____

_____

_____

_____

_____

_____

_____

BLOCK YOUR EX; NO, SERIOUSLY

Maybe things ended in a gnarly way. They broke your heart into a million pieces and kicked the shards all across your bedroom floor. Maybe they ghosted you. Or maybe it just ended in a not-so-dramatic way, painful nonetheless. Whatever the case, perhaps you're toying with the idea of blocking their number and their accounts on social media. But something is giving you pause. Would that be crazy? Over the top? Do I really need to?

The answer? Yeah, you might want to. And here's why: Blocking is for you; it's what you need to heal. It has nothing to do with the other person. It protects your energy, sets a firm boundary, and helps you move forward without being triggered by what they had for lunch on their *Instagram* story. Think about the way generations before us broke up. They didn't have constant access to their former relationships. They healed in the dark.

Keeping tabs on someone isn't healthy. Not blocking someone because you want them to see you Living Your Very Best Life also isn't healthy. It gives them the power instead of you.

Block your ex. Your mental health will thank you.

Block Your Ex

It's time to block your ex. There's no shame in doing so. Or, if you're not completely ready for the hardcore block, saving their name in your phone as *Hell No* and muting their social accounts works too.

In this space, write about what you're feeling as you get ready to block them, and afterward too.

CONTEMPLATE WHY IT DIDN'T WORK

So, it didn't work out. I'm sorry about that. I know it hurts so much right now, but it's going to be okay. But first, you're going to have to let yourself feel emotions, even the painful ones.

Sometimes, when a relationship doesn't work out, we want a damn reason. It helps us shape the narrative. Our brains like sequential stories, after all. We need a beginning, a middle, and an end. But life doesn't always work like that. In fact, most times it doesn't. And that's okay.

When you're looking back at a relationship's demise, do your best to look at it practically. Don't assign too much value to yourself or devalue your ex. Rather, look at it from a place of compatibility. Contemplate why it didn't work in terms of fit, rather than concluding you're a lost cause because you double texted them once at work in 2017 and that had to be the beginning of the end, right?

I highly doubt it.

You need to make peace with the fact that you may never have exact answers about where it went wrong. You can think back and back and back; eventually, you're going to need to move forward without all the answers. Sometimes, "It was and then it wasn't" will suffice.

Sometimes, love just ends. It runs its course. You love, and then suddenly? You don't.

That's okay.

Journal about the Major Moments

Get your contemplation on paper to see it more clearly. In the space here, write out some moments that signified the end was near. Cope with it. Be honest about how you felt then (and feel now). Get into the nitty-gritty. Be brave. It's going to be okay.

DO YOU REALLY WANT CLOSURE?

Psychology refers to "closure" in dating as knowing the exact reason behind a breakup. Human beings like stories, after all, and if we can tend to our wounds with a clear narrative, it's easier to move forward since we can label that exact moment where things fell apart. We know where the rubble lies, where it needs to be cleaned up.

Life isn't always like that, though. Neither is love.

Because there will be times when relationships end without so much as a goodbye. Whether it's through ghosting or unclear explanations, we are robbed of closure in that moment and launched into a tizzy of What the fuck just happened? For example:

> *Why did they leave?*
> *What did I do wrong?*
> *What can I do so this never happens again?*

Since it's closure we're missing, we assume that the only way we can move forward is by obtaining it from the person who decided we weren't worth it.

So we reach out. We send drunk text confessions. We're blindsided by the heartbreak. But the heartbreak refuses to move. It's as merciless as it is uncaring. So, what can we do in these moments?

Close the door ourselves.

When someone decides that their comfort and convenience matters more than our feelings, they are showing us their true colors. They're also showing us where they're at emotionally, and where they're not. They're proving we are better off without them. So, really, they gave us a gift.

Close the Door Yourself

You can close the door yourself. You can throw away the key. You can move forward without knowing their reasoning. On the following lines, write out how their silent goodbye made you feel. Get as angry, sad, and emotional as you need.

And then? Forgive them.

Yes. You heard that right. Life becomes easier when you learn to accept the apology you never got. You don't need their permission to move forward.

You only need your own. Get writing!

WHAT WILL YOU MISS NOW THAT THEY'RE GONE?

Sad fact: You're going to miss your ex. You might not want them back, but you're still going to miss what you had. Both of those things can be true. They were someone you loved once, after all; that has to count for something. Or maybe you still love them but understand you couldn't grow together any further. Whatever the case, longing for what once was is totally normal and, honestly, to be expected.

So start at the beginning. Remember the excitement of their hello. Think about the first date. The first kiss. The promise of an endless tomorrow. Then think about the annoying shit they'd do. Consider why it went wrong. Understand why you could no longer be together.

Sometimes, things break beyond repair. Put away the toolbox. Focus solely on the only piece you have left of that relationship.

And that's yourself.

Heal your wounds on your own. Let yourself feel. Move forward gently. Give yourself all the time you need. Healing is not linear. Breakups are a form of grief. Let yourself be sad. Have faith that one day, it won't hurt so much.

Journal about What You'll Miss, and What You Won't

Journal all of this as a stream of consciousness. Be honest; be vulnerable; be truthful. This is for your eyes only. This is for your healing only. You deserve to let them go.

WRITE A LETTER YOU'LL NEVER SEND TO YOUR EX

Letters you'll never send are perfect because you can be as vulnerable, honest, and brutal as you want. (You should see the Notes app on my phone; there are some absolutely *scathing* texts in there.) It's your chance to lay it all out there, process your feelings, and not worry about being judged for feeling a lil' crazy. (News flash: Pretty much no one is sane in heartbreak's wake. Just keep that to yourself; you don't want to cause collateral damage.)

So turn on the saddest breakup songs you can think of (*Folklore* by Taylor Swift?), and start writing. Embrace the pain that comes with healing. Tell them what you loved about them. What you didn't love so much. How they made you feel in the beginning. How they made you feel in the end. Share your rage. Share your hurt. Share your heart. Then, once all is said and done, print that sucker out and burn it. While burning the letter is optional, it is encouraged. It does feel symbolic. It's a way to release the heaviness of their goodbye.

Soon, there will be nothing left to hold.

Write That Letter!

Here, write the letter you are never going to send to your ex. Be specific; be real; be authentic; be whatever it is you truly feel. There are no wrong ways to express yourself. This is just for you, and your healing.

_____

_____

_____

_____

_____

_____

_____

_____

_____

_____

_____

_____

_____

_____

_____

_____

_____

_____

_____

_____

_____

DON'T LOSE YOURSELF IN SOMEONE ELSE'S STORY

They were just a character in the book of your life. Sure, you're a character in their story too, but it's just that: *theirs*. This is *your* book, baby! Stop losing yourself in their narrative.

That's in your control.

Even if you screwed up in your relationship with them, even if you're "the bad guy" in their narrative, you don't have to be in your own story. You can understand where you went wrong, sure, but you don't have to punish yourself by making yourself the villain in your narrative too. Be compassionate in the spots where you could have done better, because next time? You can.

Instead, learn from it. Allow them to be a chapter in which you learned the importance of being patient when someone was late because of work every time you'd hang out. Allow them to be the chapter in which you discovered that you need more from someone than last-minute plans.

Don't lose yourself in someone else's story, even if it was someone you loved once. Even if it was someone you'll always hold dear in your memory. You hold the pen. You get to do the writing. So, what are you waiting for?

Remind Yourself They're a Character in Your Story

Remind yourself that their story is not your story. Write a narrative about the situation from your perspective in the space provided.

THERE'S MORE TO LIFE THAN FALLING BACK IN LOVE

When heartbroken, it's easy to believe the only way to recover is to fall back in love. We think this is the only remedy.

It's not.

There is so much left to do in life besides fall back in love. You can:

★ Watch that movie you always wanted to watch
★ Travel the world
★ Find passion for your career
★ Get a dog
★ Learn a new language
★ Take your dream trip

When you finally realize that falling back in love isn't the only way to heal, your real healing will begin. Fall in love with your life. Even if no one else is by your side.

Brainstorm Other Things to Do Besides Fall Back in Love

Here, brainstorm all the things you can do besides falling back in love.
These can be hobbies, trips, career milestones, whatever!

YOU CAN MISS THEM AND NOT WANT THEM BACK

It's such an interesting feeling. You truly can miss someone and not want them back.

Just think about it. After all the hurt, all the healing, everything that went south. If they came to your door right this second and asked for you back, would you take them back? Would you hesitate? Would you be afraid?

Allow yourself to miss what was and accept that it can no longer be. It's okay to love so deeply for it only to go up in flames. It just means you're living life. You're putting your heart on the line. And that's truly so beautiful.

List Why You Wouldn't Take Them Back

In this space, list all the reasons you refuse to get back with someone who is no longer right for you. Think about reasons you're no longer compatible; consider why it had to end. Keep in mind you don't need to demonize your ex, even if they deserve a little roasting. Focus on the facts at play, and go from there.

MAYBE YOU DON'T FORGET THEM

The idea of forgetting lost love is an enticing one. *Eternal Sunshine of the Spotless Mind* digs into the idea of erasing someone from your mind. The main characters, Joel and Clementine, go through a nasty split. They undergo a neurological procedure in which their specific memories of each other are entirely wiped. I won't ruin the end if you haven't seen it, but I'll say one thing:

It doesn't go well.

Muscle memory of the heart is an interesting thing. Because even if we no longer have someone in our beds when we go to sleep at night, they are still so present in the chambers of our hearts.

Songs playing at the bar remind you of them. You pass your favorite coffee shop, your heart sinks as you remember your first date there that lasted five hours. You feel it contract and release every time someone mentions their name in conversation.

It's in these moments we long to wipe them from our memory à la *Eternal Sunshine*. The pain is as palpable as it is stubborn. It's unmoving, their absence almost drowning out all of your senses. You long for it to just stop. You begin to wish you never met them at all.

But then think about what you would have missed out on. The lessons, both good and difficult. Maybe you don't want to forget them after all. Perhaps you can't; you just get better at missing them.

One day, you'll be glad you can remember them after all.

Consider Why You'd Want to Remember Them

Write out your favorite memories and the lessons they taught you.
How did they help you grow? What did they teach you about yourself?
Consider all the reasons you'd want to remember your ex. This can
include the tough moments too. Pain is an excellent teacher at times.
Let's get to it here.

LOVE NEVER LEFT YOU; IT JUST CHANGED SHAPE

Love never left you. It's just changing shape. Okay, so what does that mean? Allow me to explain.

Just because that person's version of love walked away, doesn't mean all the types of love you have are gone. In fact, you had love before them. So, you'll have love after them too.

Love is always evolving. It doesn't leave us. It arrives in different ways over and over again. There are so many forms.

You can find love in your work. You can find love on a random Tuesday in spring when it finally starts warming up. You can find love in the pages of your favorite book. You can find love in a painting that spoke to you in ways no one else has.

You can find love in your grandparents. You can find love in your best friend. Your dog. Your immediate family.

You can find love anywhere, if you're willing to look and recognize it.

Most importantly, though, you are love too. You can give love to others and also to yourself.

Romantic love is important. This is true. It's what you want. It will happen. It will come back, usually when you least expect it. You will love again. It just might not be for a while, and that's okay. After all, love never left. It just changed shape.

Write a Love Letter to Your Life

Here, write a love letter to your best friends to remind you love exists in more ways than romance. Think about all the things you love about your life, and write them in a letter here.

_____

_____

_____

_____

_____

_____

_____

_____

_____

_____

_____

_____

_____

_____

_____

_____

_____

_____

_____

_____

_____

Chapter 6

ALMOST RELATIONSHIPS AND SITUATIONSHIPS

Understanding Undefined Relationships and How They Can Break Your Heart Too

This chapter is about letting go of someone you never had at all. That's right, we're talking almost relationships, unrequited love, and situationships. These types of relationships are so common in modern dating, in which communication is lacking and commitment is just as scarce. In addition to that, these types of romances are the most painful because they never fully took shape. But our feelings did, and that discrepancy can be hard to navigate. That's what this chapter is for. You'll learn your feelings are valid, what you felt was real. And so, you deserve to heal too.

HEARTBREAK CAN INSPIRE YOU, IF YOU LET IT

Heartbreak brought on from an almost relationship can be an excellent teacher. You learn what you're capable of. You learn what you were looking for in another person. It invites honesty. Rawness. Some goddamn real feelz!

It shows you that you could care that much for someone else, even though it was never defined. It shows you can put yourself and your heart on the line. The hurt merely shows you're human, and alive.

So what do we do with the pain? We create. Heartbreak can inspire you, if you let it. It has sparked the creativity of countless others. Demi Lovato. Ariana Grande. Adele. Look, even Beyoncé had her damn heart broken, but she turned lemons into... *Lemonade.* (BTW, heartbreak is never a reflection on your worth if Queen B goes through it!)

Heartbreak has inspired some of the greatest songs of our time. The most heart-wrenching and empowering films. The most interesting and compelling novels. The majority of the first writing I did for the Internet. There is so much to be learned from a broken heart. You can grow and evolve from being told no, from hearing not yet.

Eventually, you may find that you're grateful for the experience of the goodbye. Because now, it gives the chance for love to say hello.

List the Lessons from the Heartbreak

List out the lessons from the heartbreak. Think about everything this pain is teaching you. What will you do with it?

_____
_____
_____
_____
_____
_____
_____
_____
_____
_____
_____
_____
_____
_____
_____
_____
_____
_____
_____
_____
_____
_____
_____

YOUR HEART IS YOUR OWN TO MEND

They can't fix what they broke, but you can. You are in charge of your own well-being. You are capable of your own healing. You can move on without them, without their closure. Here's how:

Acknowledge the hurt. Stop ignoring it. It will find a way to make itself known, trust that, so face it head-on. Cry, scream, journal, write letters you'll never send, talk it out with your BFF. Whatever it takes, feel that pain.

Figure out what story you're telling yourself about this particular heartbreak. Are you putting them on a pedestal? Are you using them as proof that you suck? You can be heartbroken and disappointed it didn't work out because you really liked them; you should never give their inability to love you as proof of unworthiness. If you are, this is your chance to reroute that thought.

Take breaks from it. See your friends and focus on them. Go for a sweaty run. Call your mom and ask about her day. Throw yourself into work or an exciting new personal project.

Whatever you do, don't turn to the person who broke your heart. It's easy to text and want to ask questions or demand closure. But this is scratching an open wound. Please, don't do it.

Put the pieces back together yourself. They belong to you.

It's going to take effort. It's not just waiting for the hurt to go away; it's helping the healing process along too.

Put the Pieces Back Together Yourself

It's time to put your pieces back together yourself. Think about how this person might have broken something in you. For example, maybe they made you believe everyone leaves. In the space provided, write out the broken belief, and then write out why this isn't true and how you'll mend that belief yourself.

_____

_____

_____

_____

_____

_____

_____

_____

_____

_____

_____

_____

_____

_____

_____

_____

_____

_____

_____

DON'T CHANGE YOURSELF SO THEY'LL LOVE YOU BACK

Unrequited love is one of the most painful experiences. Most people go through it at one point or another. But that doesn't make it feel less difficult or less lonely. In fact, it's one of the loneliest loves there is.

Beyond being lonely, unrequited love can trick you into thinking that you're not enough or, maybe worse, that you're way too much. You start listing your faults, thinking of all the ways you surely pushed them away. You contemplate how you can change so maybe, just maybe, you can win them over. And maybe, just maybe, they'll finally love you back.

Pro tip: Don't do this. It never works.

Because let's say you do morph into some version of yourself that they end up falling for. For a while, you might feel as if you've won. You might feel validated. You got them. Eventually, though, you'll get tired of pretending. You'll grow sick of acting chill when inside you're screaming.

Why not just be you, and find someone who loves you for that too? Don't betray yourself by thinking everything that you are is what makes you unlovable. No. It just means you weren't right for this particular person. And in the end, that means they weren't right for you either.

You don't want who doesn't want you. Full stop.

Unrequited love isn't your final destination. It's just a stop along the way. It will help you learn to understand what you deserve: someone who loves you back for you.

Write a Poem about Unrequited Love

In this space, write a poem about your unrequited love. Honor everything you felt; remember the moments that were good and the moments that broke your heart too. Expressing your pain is a helpful way to move through it.

FALL OUT OF LOVE WITH THE IDEA OF THEM

The most dangerous thing to fall in love with is an idea. (Actually, it's probably people named Travis, but that's a conversation for another time.) But ideas are a close second. Here's why:

Ideas are full of potential. When we meet someone who seemingly checks all of our boxes, we cling to that list. We see possibility in the way they laugh. We project our own wants and needs. We ascribe meaning to moments that maybe didn't mean anything at all. We construct a narrative based on what we already believe about them: They're wonderful.

But potential doesn't always see itself through. It's weightless in its hope. Sometimes, it's never fully actualized, leaving nothing but pain in its wake.

We've all fallen in love with an idea before. They are saying what we want to hear. They look like the real thing, and you're so excited. For the first time in a long while, you're thinking, Damn, maybe this is who I've finally been looking for.

But then, reality settles in.

They stop calling. They start exhibiting behavior that deviates from what you expected. You realize what you wanted to hear was just that— what you *wanted* to hear, not what they were actually saying. Eventually, it all falls apart, and it's up to you to pick up your own pieces.

That part always sucks, but it will make you stronger. Your heart is resilient. And recovering from heartbreak is a skill like any other; you get better at it every time.

Compare Ideas to Reality

In the following space, make two columns. In the first column, reflect on who you thought they were. Be as specific as possible. Don't be afraid to be honest. Then, in the second column, write the facts. Say who they ended up *actually* being, as a person and as a partner.

SOON, THEY'LL JUST BE SOMEONE YOU ONCE LOVED

If you want to let them go, paint over your rose-gold memories with truth.

Look a little closer. It's then that you'll see their eyes were never two shots of whiskey; they were just brown. You'll understand they weren't a soul mate; they were just someone you loved once. Heartbreak becomes easier to carry when you allow yourself to remember someone as they actually were, not the person you wanted them to be.

Of course, it's not that simple, especially when it comes to an almost relationship that grew to be love. But if you look at the pain as temporary (which it very much is), it might be easier to see light at the end of the tunnel. You'll understand that healing is possible, and just on the horizon.

Soon, they'll just be someone you used to love. Soon, they'll be a lesson. Soon, they'll be your past. Soon, they will be someone you might realize you never really knew that well at all.

You will move on. You will hurt first, but you will let them go. You can trust that better things are coming. And that's a love that truly loves you back. Someone who will commit to you. Someone you are meant to be with, long term.

Explain Who They Were to You

In the space here, explain exactly who this person was to you. Were they your first love, who turned into your first heartbreak? Were they your favorite person to go on random drives with? Did they hold space for you, even if those moments weren't made for longevity? Be honest; be vulnerable; be real; after all, what you felt was. Why not be honest too?

_____

_____

_____

_____

_____

_____

_____

_____

_____

_____

_____

_____

_____

_____

_____

_____

_____

_____

♥ YOUR FEELINGS WERE REAL

Sometimes, you won't get the closure you deserve. The apology you long for. The breakup that never was because the relationship never came to fully be.

The trouble with processing an almost relationship's end is that you convince yourself what you had with the other person was never "real." They never committed to you, right? You never committed to them, perhaps because you never made your feelings known. Maybe it was because you claimed you were okay with the ambiguity.

Whatever the case, there's no anniversary to be remembered. The beginning, middle, and end all blurred together to paint one gray "WTF was that?" picture.

It's easy to dismiss that pain since it wasn't technically a relationship. We never even dated, you keep thinking. How could I possibly feel this way?

It was real, though. Your feelings were valid. Just because it wasn't a serious relationship doesn't mean it wasn't a relationship of some sort. You meant something to them, and they meant something to you. Just because it didn't become something defined and long-lasting doesn't mean it didn't count. It doesn't mean you can't be grateful that it happened. It doesn't mean you didn't learn a thing or two. It doesn't mean you can't be sad when it finally ends, which it always does.

To let go, honor your feelings. When you do this, you start to accept it too. You look back and start to appreciate them for what they were, and weren't. You move through it. And then? You move on.

Honor Your Feelings

In this exercise, you're going to be as vulnerable as possible about an almost relationship. In each statement, fill in the blank about your own situation. This is just for you, remember. Feel whatever it is you feel. Name it. Honor it. Accept it. Let it go.

I almost had you, but _____

_____ got in the way.

I wish we got to _____

_____,

but I now understand that we were _____

_____.

We had a chance, but it wasn't _____

_____

_____.

I know I miss you now, and one day I _____

_____

_____.

I will honor my feelings now so I can move forward to _____

_____

_____.

I deserve that much. I deserve more than an almost _____

_____

_____.

GIVE YOURSELF THE CHANCE THEY NEVER GAVE YOU

Almost relationships are hella painful due to their lack of shape. While we're making our way through their aftermath, we often are upset because time feels wasted. We start to wonder how we could have felt something so deep, so honest, for someone else who we never even got to call our S.O. Why did we spend so much time on someone who is no longer saved in our phones? Or, if you're me, you save each one as a ghost emoji or *Don't Even Answer*.

Here's the thing, though: You can learn a lot from the ones who only end up being an almost. In all the spaces they leave behind, we get the chance to fill in the blanks. We get to give ourselves the chance they never gave us.

In a way, almost relationships are a ton of opportunities wrapped into one experience. Almost relationships teach us we deserve some-one consistent. They reveal how maybe we ask for less than we want because we think that's all we deserve. We slowly come to understand sometimes the person we want doesn't want us back. And we figure out how to be okay with that.

So give yourself the chance they never gave you. Work on yourself, for yourself. Put yourself out there when you're ready. Understand they weren't the one you'd spend your days with, but they were worth the lesson.

Sometimes, what you learn from the fall is worth the bruise.

Thank Your Almost Relationship

In the candy hearts, for each "Thank you," fill in the rest. For example: "Thank you for teaching me what I deserve" or "Thank you for helping me learn to love myself, even though you couldn't."

Chapter 7

FINDING THE REAL THING

Falling in Love, Getting Married, and Committing Long Term

This is the part about finding the real thing. The person you want to stay with. Your future partner fo lyfe. Hell yeah! This chapter will invite you to imagine your dream wedding (if that's your thing), share all the lovely ways you'll show up for your partner in the years to come, and inspire you to keep romance alive. Committing to someone else means putting in the work and effort. This chapter will remind you of just that.

YOUR PERSON MAKES PERFECT SENSE, IF YOU LOOK BACK

Everything that happened in your life so far has led to this current moment. Every move. Every career change. Every decision you've made. Every wrong turn. There is no room for "should-have-been" or "could-have-been" here, only what is.

This should bring you a sense of peace. Everything is as it should be. This comes down to your partner too. Everything in your life so far has led you to them.

What if the person in college never ghosted you? Then you'd probably have told your now S.O. no when they asked you to dance the following weekend at the bar. What if you stayed in that shitty relationship even another week? Maybe you'd still be healing by the time you first flirted with your partner at the coffee shop.

Beyond these things, though, think about it from the perspective of fate. They happened to go to your college or frequent the same bars you do or even have the same friends you have. They entered your atmosphere not by chance but on purpose.

Looking back, you should feel a sense of gratitude and joy. Allow yourself to ponder how damn lucky you got to exist at the same time they were human too. How they stood by your side through the tough moments and the happy ones too. How compatible you are goes beyond chemistry.

You need to connect the dots if you're not seeing this yet. You'll be so glad you did.

Connect the Dots

In this space, write out all the major events that led you to your person.
Think about where you met them. How you met them. How you were in
the right place mentally. Write it all out here.

_____

_____

_____

_____

_____

_____

_____

_____

_____

_____

_____

_____

_____

_____

_____

_____

_____

_____

_____

_____

_____

_____

REMEMBER IT *CAN* BE DIFFICULT (BUT IT *SHOULDN'T* BE HARD)

When I started writing this book, I consulted my BFF about what has made her marriage work. She said the following, and I think it's damn good advice:

It can be difficult, sure, but it shouldn't be hard.

(Given that my BFF is a Scorpio queen, believe me when I say you should heed her advice. She's right pretty much 99.999 percent of the time.)

Life is and always will be difficult. Your relationship shouldn't be one of the things that makes this true. Your relationship should be your safe space. Your S.O. should challenge you intellectually. They should encourage your growth. They should show you various ways to see things.

The challenge they shouldn't be giving you is disrespect. Putting up with walls that should have come down a long time ago. Being unkind. Cruel. Annoying you on purpose. Pushing your boundaries. That's not someone worth being with. That's the wrong fit.

So, remember during the tough moments, it's just a *moment*. Remember what you love about the relationship as a whole. Remember why you fell in love with them in the first place and why you're in it for the long run. Choose them every day. Keep in mind why you do so.

List How They Challenge You

In the space provided, write out how your partner challenges you. Think about how they expand your horizons, encourage you to think differently, and may even push your buttons a little.

ASK THESE DEEP QUESTIONS TO BRING YOU AND YOUR PARTNER CLOSER

Icebreakers aren't just for the beginnings of a partnership; they're for all the other parts too. Ask your partner some of the following questions when you're looking for something new to talk about:

★ What is something you like about yourself?
★ What is something you don't like about yourself?
★ What does love feel like to you?
★ What is your favorite word?
★ When was the last time you were joyous?
★ What is something about yourself that you feel goes unnoticed?
★ Do you feel appreciated by me?
★ What's the first thing you noticed about me?
★ What are the first signs that you know you're in love?
★ Why me?

Some other ways to bond with your partner include conversation starters like We're Not Really Strangers, a card game designed to bring people closer. Seek out new experiences, ask the tough questions, learn about their inner world—it keeps things interesting.

Come Up with Your Own Questions

A good relationship is one in which you're always learning, about yourself and the other person. Asking questions is the perfect way to get to know your partner even better than you already do. Silly, deep, profound, or out-of-body are all on the table. Think of some questions to ask your S.O. in the following space.

REMEMBER THIS: YOUR PERSON ISN'T YOUR EVERYTHING

Your person isn't your everything. They're not the only person in your life. You have your nonromantic soul mates to love too.

As mentioned in Chapter 2, taking time apart is one of the key components of fostering a healthy relationship. Keeping in mind you are your own person and they are their own person is crucial.

The right person for you will not complete your life. They will add to it. Expand it. Make it a little more fun.

You want someone who is part of your world but not the whole damn universe. You have your own goals and aspirations outside of marriage, right? Keep those in mind. Work toward personal goals too. Make time for your friends still. Call your grandparents (you'll miss it when you can't one day, trust me). Call your parents too, while you're at it.

Your person isn't your everything. But they are a big something. Just make sure you're approaching your relationship from a balanced place. It's much healthier that way.

List Ways You'll Spend Time Apart from Your Person

Here, list some adventures you'll embark on without your partner. These can be done with your family, friends, or colleagues, or by yourself. For example: happy hour margs on Tuesdays with your BFFs, a conference with your work friend, or Sunday dinner at your parents' place.

FIND THE ROMANCE IN ROUTINE

Romance is great, but it's who you want to run to Home Depot with on a Sunday afternoon who is the right person for you.

Think about who you'd enjoy grocery shopping with. The person who you could build IKEA furniture with (without filing for divorce). The person who helps you draft emails. The person who helps you pick out jeans that make your butt look damn good. Think about someone who you could paint a living room with. Who you could do home renovation projects with. Who you could have fun doing *anything* with.

Think about who you want to spend Sunday with. Who you want to come home to Monday night. Think about the person you want to wake up next to and not mind their messy bed head. Saturday is date night, but Sunday is real life. Saturday is red wine; Sunday is coffee and reading the paper in comfortable silence.

Romance is important, but the real-life moments matter just as much. In fact, they might even matter more.

Take some time to think about how you will find romance in routine. How will you find cute moments in your daily life?

Brainstorm Nonromantic Dates

On the following lines, brainstorm some nonromantic "dates" you and your partner can embark on. Think about home projects, athletic activities, and other events. Include errands on the list too. Then, write out ways you'll make the mundane fun.

♥ LOVE IS A VERB

Think about this: How can you say "I love you" without saying those three little words? Love is beyond the word. It's the action. The intention. The effort. It's not what you say you do, it's what you actually do that counts. I sound like a living, breathing *Pinterest* board, but clichés exist for a reason, do they not? They're universal truths that relate to most walks of life.

So how can you say "I love you" with your behavior? How about breakfast in bed? Making sure the refrigerator is stocked with their favorite beer or wine? Writing little love notes and leaving them on their desk? Asking them if they want to go to Target (that's the sixth love language).

Speaking of love languages, knowing your partner's is a great way to learn how to express love in a way they'll understand. Ask your partner if they know theirs (or have them take a quiz). Once they have an answer, brainstorm ways to show them love in that love language.

When it comes down to it, actions do speak louder than words. Show, don't tell, your partner your love.

List Ways to Say "I Love You" Without Actually Saying It

So now that you understand that love is a verb, it's time to put this to the test. In the following space, list out all the ways you can show your partner you love them without literally saying "I love you."

★ _____
★ _____
★ _____
★ _____
★ _____
★ _____
★ _____
★ _____
★ _____
★ _____
★ _____
★ _____
★ _____
★ _____
★ _____
★ _____
★ _____
★ _____
★ _____
★ _____

❤ YOU, THEM, AND US

A family friend once told me that a relationship has three components. There's you, there's the other person, and then there's the "couple" part; all three need to be their own entities to function well as a unit.

This is to say: You are your own before anyone else's. They were their own before they were yours. And the relationship came to be because you both decided life would be a lot more fun if you experienced it all together, as a team.

It's helpful to think of relationships this way because it encourages balance and individual identities outside of each other. It also holds space for the fact that, yes, your relationship is its own thing and deserves nurturing and care too.

Remember how self-love is imperative, no matter what your relationship status is? This is where this comes into practice.

Nurture each of these components so the entire unit works well as a whole. Pay attention when things get tough and acknowledge which part of you, them, or us might be lagging. Then, nurture it. Pay attention to what needs healing or tending to.

And then, get to work.

Fill Out the "You, Them, Us" Venn Diagram

In the following Venn diagram, write in some identifying features of each component of your own relationship. For example:

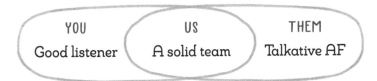

YOU
Good listener

US
A solid team

THEM
Talkative AF

Be as thorough as possible.

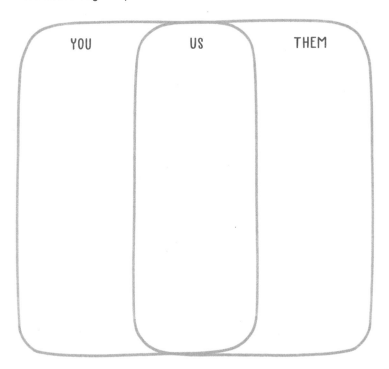

YOU

US

THEM

HOLD SPACE FOR YOUR PARTNER

Holding space is an act of love. It's not fixing your S.O.'s problems but giving them enough room to figure it out on their own (or lending a helping hand when necessary and appropriate).

You can't save anyone. You can only love them. People are not projects. They are not there for you to reshape into something you want. Instead of trying to repair what you didn't break, hold space. Listen. You are a supporter; you are not a savior. They are your partner, not your job.

Please don't judge their situation or try to fix it. Instead, practice loving-kindness. Actively listen, not just to respond but to understand.

You're not meant to heal your partner. You can only love them. Be there. Show up consistently. That is your role, nothing more and nothing less. And that's what it means to hold space.

It takes courage to do this, but so does loving. So, trust that you are capable of holding space for your partner. You love them, after all. Holding space is just the next step.

Hold Space for Your Partner in These Unique Ways

In the following space, list some ways you think you can hold space for your partner. Think of specific scenarios in which this might be necessary, such as a bad day at work or a fight with their best friend.

♥ DRAFT YOUR VOWS

So, you've found the one you wanna marry. *Cue that one viral Bruno Mars's song that still lives rent-free in my head!* I'm totally thrilled for you. No, seriously, I love love. I don't know you, but I'm so happy you get to embark on such a wonderful journey with another person.

Committing to someone long term is super scary, especially in our noncommittal culture. You know the divorce rate. You understand nothing in life is guaranteed. But this human you've found, your partner, is worth taking this leap of faith with. You believe you two could create a hell of a life. You're prepared to give them your all. You're ready.

Marriage is leaning into hope rather than fear. After all, without a little wishful thinking, love would never even have a chance to begin, let alone last.

So when you get up there to do the thing and put a ring on it, what are you going to say to your spouse? What do you want them to know? How do you want to profess your love to them in front of your friends and family? Now, it'll be easy to overthink this. It's a big moment, after all, one of the biggest of your life!

Remember the first date, the first time you told them you loved them, your first fight, your favorite memories, your most cherished parts of them. Reflect on all the ways love snuck into your life. Think about how happy you are it arrived in the person you plan to spend forever alongside.

Write Those Vows

Here, write out all the ways you're committing to your partner. Share what you love about them. How you'll love them every single day. What made you fall in love with them in the first place. How you'll show your commitment in ways other than a ring on your finger. How you'll stand by their side in good times, and difficult.

_____

_____

_____

_____

_____

_____

_____

_____

_____

_____

_____

_____

_____

_____

_____

_____

_____

_____

THINK OF WAYS TO KEEP IT FRESH

It's okay to become comfortable in a relationship. It's a good thing when this happens! What *isn't* so great is becoming complacent and taking your relationship for granted. You need to keep your partnership alive through nurture, love, and novel experiences.

Of course, this isn't to say you can make love feel like utter excitement at all times. Nah, sometimes it's gonna be a little boring. You will fall into a routine together. This is totally normal and not a sign of a stale relationship. However, you *are* going to want to shake things up every so often to keep it fresh and find new ways to appreciate one another.

One way to do this is by practicing gratitude. As often as you can, look at your partner in the morning and remind yourself how lucky you are they are in your life. How happy you are they chose you, and you chose them.

Another way to keep it fresh is by being spontaneous. Take an impromptu road trip on the weekend. Call in "sick" to work together and make brunch at home. (Mimosas optional but encouraged.) Dance in the kitchen even though there's nothing to celebrate. Toast to each other every night. The options are endless.

Most importantly, though, find ways to make the little moments fun. Make going to the grocery store a party. Blast new music together while you share your weekly chores. Whatever is routine, find a way to make it more special.

This is where the good stuff resides.

List How You Will Keep the Romance Spark Lit

List out all the ways you can keep your relationship fresh. Breakfast in bed? Yearly trips? Shared hobbies? Don't be afraid to think out of the box.

★ _____
★ _____
★ _____
★ _____
★ _____
★ _____
★ _____
★ _____
★ _____
★ _____
★ _____
★ _____
★ _____
★ _____
★ _____
★ _____
★ _____
★ _____
★ _____

IMAGINE YOUR DREAM WEDDING

I have always wanted a wedding, though I've been way too embarrassed to admit it. I mean, hell, I have a *Pinterest* wedding board set to "Secret" because it felt so silly to think about an event that might not even happen. But I'm starting to have a change of heart. Dreams never hurt anyone, after all, and it's fun to think about.

If you want to get married, own it. It's okay to want to celebrate your love with everyone closest to you and your partner.

So think about what your dream wedding would entail. Think about who you want there. Think as big as possible too. And, while you're at it, create a *Pinterest* board for more inspiration. But don't set it to "Private." Own it.

It's okay to want a wedding! It doesn't make you weak. It makes you human. Allow yourself to feel the joy of love and partnership.

Also, if you don't want a wedding, that's *okay*. You don't need to.

But you need to celebrate your love in some way. It deserves some attention, even if it's just you and your spouse acknowledging the union. You don't have to drop $15K.

Love is always worth celebrating. Be happy you found it. You deserve it.

Plan Your Dream Wedding

Weddings are a beautiful celebration of love. If a wedding is something you want too, this is your chance to plan. Build your dream wedding with help from the following prompts. Be as specific as possible.

Who would be in your wedding party?

_____

What would you wear?

_____

What season do you want to wed in?

_____

Where would you get married?

_____

DJ or band?

_____

Who would give toasts?

_____

Would you write your own vows or nah?

_____

What would your first dance song be? Do you even want one?

_____

What are special details you'd need to have?

_____

♡ SHOW UP FOR LOVE

Love that's meant for you always stays, but you *do* have to show up in order to experience it. You need to allow yourself to be available for its warmth. You need to make an effort. You need to do the work.

Showing up for love takes vulnerability. Courage. Hope. Commitment.

Besides receiving love, how are you going to give love? What are the little ways you will let your partner know how much you care? How excited are you that they chose you over anyone else they could have done life with?

Stop waiting for love to leave. It's here to stay, if you are willing to show it some hospitality. You need to nurture it. Fuel it. Feed it. But, mostly, you need to have some faith in it.

Love, in the end, is all we have. It's why we're here. It's what we're meant to do.

If the world needs anything, it needs more love. It needs people committed to caring for each other. That energy, that hopefulness, it's contagious, really. It gives others permission to be a little too much, love a little too hard, be a little cringe.

The more we allow ourselves to be seen, the more we allow ourselves to be loved. And the more we exemplify this, the more courage others will have to do the same.

So, my one wish for you is that you choose it every single day. I hope you show up for love. You deserve that much.

List the Ways You'll Show Up for Love

List all the ways you'll show up for love. How you'll fill your own cup and your partner's. How you will share your love with the world, while you're at it. For example: "I will show up for love by sticking to my values" or "I will think of little ways to show them I'm theirs" or "I will bring them coffee during tough workweeks."

★ _____

★ _____

★ _____

★ _____

★ _____

★ _____

★ _____

★ _____

★ _____

ABOUT THE AUTHOR

MOLLY BURFORD is a wellness writer based in southeastern Michigan. She mostly covers relationships and mental health, including both reported and personal pieces on modern dating, sexuality, mental illness, cannabis, and more. Her work has been featured in *Allure*, *Cosmopolitan*, *Glamour*, *Teen Vogue*, *Thought Catalog*, *Greatist*, *Self*, and *The Financial Diet*, among others. She is also the author of *The No Worries Workbook*, *Say Yes to Yourself*, and *The DIY Bucket List*, all published by Adams Media, an imprint of Simon & Schuster.

Molly became a writer because she could never find a way to shut up. As such, writing seemed to be the best way to channel the constant chatter she felt the need to share. Therapy also helped. Mostly, though, Molly became a writer in hopes that by sharing her personal stories about dating and mental health, she could help someone else feel less alone and more understood. Molly firmly believes we've been put on this earth to connect, and her route to connection just happened to be through the written word.

When she's not oversharing online, Molly can be found telling dad jokes, hanging out with her rescue dog, Bruce, making an obscene amount of Spotify playlists, and hanging out with family and friends.

Follow Molly on *Instagram* @mollyburford, on *Twitter* @mburf92, or visit her website at MollyBurford.com.